Science Fair Projects

Middle School

By
Loraine Hoffman and Greg Phillips

Cover Design by
Jeff Van Kanegan

Inside Illustrations by
Janet Armbrust

Published by Instructional Fair • TS Denison
an imprint of

 **Children's Publishing**

Authors: Loraine Hoffman and Greg Phillips
Cover Design: Jeff Van Kanegan
Inside Illustrations: Janet Armbrust
Photo Credits: McGraw-Hill Children's Publishing

 Children's Publishing

Published by Instructional Fair • TS Denison
An imprint of McGraw-Hill Children's Publishing
Copyright © 1997 McGraw-Hill Children's Publishing

Send all inquiries to:
McGraw-Hill Children's Publishing
3195 Wilson Drive NW
Grand Rapids, Michigan 49544

Science Fair Projects—middle school
ISBN: 1-56822-429-X

4 5 6 7 8 9 PHXBK 08 07 06 05 04 03

The McGraw-Hill Companies

Table of Contents

Introduction

Holding a science fair is a great way for students to begin to explore scientific inquiry through hands-on projects.

The most noticeable difference in science fair contests from school to school is the level of competition. While this will vary, the key is that students are learning to ask questions using the scientific method. The science fair is intended to expose school-aged students to the wonders of science in the world around them. It is hoped that this will encourage a pursuit of science through their school years and beyond. Experiments usually extend over a period of weeks, teaching students patience in the proper collection and evaluation of scientific data.

Some schools may hold school-wide science fairs, while other schools may have winners advancing to district, area, regional, and state competitions. Whether the science fair is a local contest or a widely advanced competition, students are learning the steps of the scientific method by engaging in real scientific experiments.

Science fairs are fun and exciting, yet each year preparations for the science fair present both teachers and students with decisions to make. Teachers have to consider how to determine and assign projects. Teachers and students must also consider the most effective presentation for projects.

Most of this book is directed at providing ideas for students and their teachers who are looking for science fair project ideas. Each science experiment in this book is presented in step-by-step procedures using the scientific method. This approach will allow students to carry out the experiment and learn and appreciate the scientific method.

There are many ways to choose experiments for the science fair. One of the most important activities for the class is brainstorming. This procedure enables the teacher to find out what interests students and discover what they are curious about. Any topic from plants, cars, and bugs to electricity and music should be recorded in class. Next, involve the class in thinking of questions about the topics. This brainstorming process begins to generate excitement and anticipation about the science fair, as well as to help students focus on their own preferred area of study. This book will provide experiments and ideas that students can use as they develop their science fair projects.

Students can choose experiments from this book during individual conferences with the teacher or by viewing copies of all the experiments from this book made available by the teacher. This allows the teacher to highlight the interests of each student and for students to make their own choices about their projects.

Once students have chosen their experiments, they should read them thoroughly, developing questions and considering potential problems. Students should have a clear concept of what they are attempting to do in the experiment. Once students are busy working on the projects, they can carry them out with minor supervision. The projects in this book are designed so that students should be able to do them largely on their own. The teacher is a resource person and can answer questions or help reason through a difficult step, but the student is the experimenter and will learn the most from the effort.

A catalog ordering information page is included in the back of the book for items that are not readily available. Students are typically responsible for the cost of their materials.

A presentation page is also included in this book. This is especially important when students get ready for the actual science fair. An experiment can be done to perfection if a student's knowledge and understanding are excellent. However, if the materials are poorly displayed, the project will not receive the recognition it deserves.

SCIENTIFIC METHOD

The scientific method is a step-by-step procedure which is used to determine the answer to a scientific question. There are six steps involved in the scientific method.

1. <u>Problem</u>: The problem is stated in a clear and concise manner.

2. <u>Hypothesis</u>: The hypothesis is an educated guess which provides a direction to the experimental process. A hypothesis can be proved or disproved.

3. <u>Materials</u>: The materials stated will include all the items that are needed for the experiment.

4. <u>Procedure</u>: The procedure lists a step-by-step explanation of the experimental process with appropriate detail.

5. <u>Results</u>: The results should be written in the form of observations.

6. <u>Conclusion</u>: The conclusion is drawn by looking at the results and comparing them with the problem. The results must be interpreted to answer the question.

What is the importance of the scientific method?

The scientific method allows a scientist to use a logical problem-solving approach to answer a question. If the scientist encounters a problem, or the experiment fails, the scientific method will provide clues or remedies to make logical changes in the experiment. In the past, before the scientific method was employed, experimenters used trial and error. This often led to repetition of experiments, misleading results, and incorrect conclusions.

Another important aspect of the scientific method is that it allows a scientist to repeat or replicate another scientist's experiment. If the experiment cannot be replicated, then the conclusions drawn from the original experiment are suspect and questioned. So the scientific method provides a framework for experiments and conclusions to be replicated.

For example, the recent cold fusion controversy revolved around not being able to replicate experiments or conclusions. One group of scientists claimed they were able to create fusion, a high energy source, at room temperature, which was thought to be impossible. Both the scientific community, as well as the public, were excited about the prospects of this enormous new energy source. However, as other scientists around the nation and the world tried to repeat these experiments, they were unable to do so.

THE BAFFLING BRIDGE CROSSING

The purpose of this activity is to engage in a brief exercise to illustrate the scientific method. In this simulation, students must use all the steps of the scientific method to solve the problem in "The Baffling Bridge Crossing." The problem is how to get a goat, a wolf, and a bale of hay across a bridge one at a time using a wheelbarrow without one item eating another item. If left alone, the goat will eat the hay, or the wolf might eat the goat!

This simulation works best when done individually over a period of about 20 minutes. Then the teacher should review the activity with the full group to prompt responses and discuss solutions.

There are several possible solutions to this problem. One solution is easily explained by taking the goat across the bridge first. Next, pick up the hay and take it across. Drop the hay off on the other side and load the goat back into the wheelbarrow. Return the goat to the original side and load the wolf. Take the wolf to the other side to be with the hay. Finally, go back for the goat and place the goat on the other side with the wolf and the hay.

Briefly, the steps to solving the problem using the scientific method begin by stating the problem. Students will write a statement like, "The problem is how to get the three items over the bridge using the wheelbarrow without one item being eaten by another item." Next, the *hypothesis*, which is an educated guess, can be stated in positive or negative terms. For example, "It is possible to transport all three items to the other side of the bridge without one item eating another item." Third, the materials used to complete the procedures needed for the experiment must be recorded. Students must make a list of all the materials they used. This list may vary from student to student, depending upon how they solved the problem. However, everyone should include a goat, a wolf, a bale of hay, a bridge, and a wheelbarrow. Fourth, students must record the procedures used to complete the experiment. For example, they must record who was carried across the bridge first, second, and third. Students should take special care to correctly record the sequence of events in the procedure. Then, students must record the results of the experiment. The results include any observations made during the experiment, such as the length of time taken to accomplish the task or what the other items were doing while an item was being transported. Finally, students must write their conclusions from the experiment. The conclusion(s) is the answer to the stated problem, including how it was accomplished.

This activity can be done either in groups or individually. In groups, students may think of more creative ways to accomplish the task. In addition, allow for greater creativity by permitting students to use other items that they may reasonably have with them to accomplish the task. Students will also enjoy the challenge of the teacher timing the groups to determine which group can accomplish the task first. The teacher can record the length of time spent by each group and may also find the average length of time taken per class and compare classes.

Solve the following problem by using the six steps of the scientific method. Explain each step thoroughly in the spaces given.

The Circumstances

You are on one side of a narrow stone bridge with a wolf, a goat, and a bale of hay. You must try to move all three across the narrow bridge using your wheelbarrow. Unfortunately, only one item can fit in your wheelbarrow at a time. To add to the problem, if left alone, the goat will eat the hay. Even worse, if left together, the wolf will eat the goat.

The first step in scientific method is the *statement of the problem*. Given the circumstances above, state the problem in your own words.

Problem: _____

_____

_____

_____

The second step in the scientific method is the *hypothesis*. State the hypothesis for solving the problem. In other words, is it possible to get all three items across the bridge?

Hypothesis: _____

_____

_____

_____

The third step in the scientific method is *materials*. List the materials needed to accomplish this task.

Materials: _____

_____

_____

_____

The fourth step in the scientific method is the *procedure*. State the step-by-step procedure to successfully complete this task.

Procedure: _____

_____

_____

_____

_____

_____

_____

_____

_____

_____

The fifth step in the scientific method is *recording results*. Results are recorded observations or data collected by the scientist during the time of experimentation. In this particular example, some observations might be the time required to complete the task or the activity of the two items left alone as the other item was transported.

Results: _____

_____

_____

_____

The sixth step in the scientific method is the *conclusion*. The conclusion is the answer or answers to the stated problem. State the conclusion(s) to the stated problem.

Conclusion: _____

_____

_____

_____

SOLVING SPHERES

This activity also allows students to solve a problem using the scientific method. To accomplish the task set forth in this experiment, students must understand the definition of the term *diameter*. Encourage students to consult their math text, science text, or dictionary.

In the statement of the problem, students can write, "What is the diameter of the space rock (Styrofoam ball)?" Second, the hypothesis must be stated in either positive or negative terms. Students may write, "The space rock will fit in the astronaut's bag." Next, students must list any materials used to complete the experiment. The materials may vary according to how students solve the problem. Fourth, students must record their procedure in a step-by-step fashion. Fifth, the results must be recorded, including all values used to determine the diameter. Finally, students must draw a conclusion(s) which answers the problem. That is, did the space rock fit into the astronaut's bag?

Next, distribute Styrofoam balls to students, asking them to find the diameter for the reasons explained in the circumstances set forth in this activity. Students may work individually or in small groups to accomplish this task. It is fun if the teacher has a bag available so students can check their conclusions by placing their "space rocks"into the "astronaut's bag."

There are several solutions to solving this problem. One is to place the ball against a ruler and measure its height. The height measured is the same value as the diameter. Another solution is to place two tips of a compass on either side of the ball. Next, measure the distance between the two tips of the compass by placing it on a ruler. Mathematically, a solution can be attained by using the formula circumference equals π (3.14) times the diameter. The circumference can be found by wrapping a string all the way around the ball and measuring its length. Remember to divide by π (3.14) to attain the answer.

Solve the problem below using the scientific method. Explain each step thoroughly in the space below.

The Circumstances

Imagine that you are an astronaut collecting rock samples. The diameter of the opening of your bag is only so large. You have found a wonderful rock for the collection, but you need to determine the diameter of your rock to see whether it will fit through the opening of your bag.

Envision the Styrofoam ball you have been given as your space rock. It is your responsibility to determine the diameter of the ball. There are a number of ways to solve the problem. Use your creativity to discover a method for solving this problem.

In some cases initial research is needed to answer a question. In this case, the scientist must understand what the term *diameter* means in order to accomplish the necessary tasks.

Using an accessible resource, look up the definition of *diameter*. Write the definition in the following space.

_____

_____

_____

The first step in the scientific method is the statement of the problem. Given the circumstances above, state the problem in your own words.

Problem:_____

_____

_____

_____

The second step in the scientific method is the statement of the hypothesis. In this case, use your best judgment to speculate whether the rock will fit into the bag. State your hypothesis in the space below.

Hypothesis: _____

_____

_____

_____

The third step in the scientific method is materials. List the materials that are needed or used in the space below.

Materials: _____

_____

_____

_____

The fourth step in the scientific method is procedure. List the steps you used in the order in which you accomplished them.

Procedure: _____

_____

_____

_____

_____

_____

The fifth step in the scientific method is results. Record any numerical values that you found. Be certain to include the appropriate unit of measure, such as inches or centimeters.

Results: _____

_____

_____

_____

The final step in the scientific method is conclusions. The conclusion(s) is the answer to the stated problem. Use the space below to state the conclusion(s).

Conclusions: _____

_____

_____

_____

_____

CHECKING-IN CREEPY CRAWLERS

Does your school have bugs? How many? Where? What kind? This can be determined by doing a demographic study at your school!

A *demographic study* is the study of populations. Demographic studies are surveys of living organisms, either plants or animals. These surveys are usually done for the purpose of determining how many organisms exist in a certain area. Demographic surveys also explore preferred habitats of animals, food preferences, and sources.

Scientists do demographic studies just about everywhere. Some are done on land while others are done in water. Conservationists and wildlife officials, for example, are very interested to find out about deer, dove, or quail populations. Studies done in water will discover which types of fish are present, along with their approximate numbers. This kind of information can be used to determine hunting and fishing limits, and can provide important information for restocking fish and wildlife. Over the years these kinds of studies have provided environmentalists with important information for the reestablishment, resurgence, and increased numbers of many wildlife populations.

Demographic studies investigating insect populations also provide health officials with needed information. Insects can cause damage to health, homes, and agriculture. Health officials use demographic information to determine if any disease-carrying mosquitoes exist in a particular area. This will help them control the mosquitoes by concentrating their spraying patterns. In California, the Mediterranean Fruit Fly has devastated citrus crops, as well as other cash crops. By using demographic surveys, the scientists can determine where to concentrate their control efforts to prevent the spread of this pest. Throughout the southern United States, the fire ant and more recently, the killer bee have been studied to find an effective means for halting their spread to other portions of the United States.

Research

1. Investigate the term *demographics* to develop an understanding of all that the term entails.

2. Select an insect in your native area to research. Be certain to give attention to the time of year and season when various insects are abundant. Three possibilities are roaches, ants, or fruit flies.

PROBLEM

Imagine that your school is experiencing a pest problem. To provide the most effective method of pest control, it is necessary to know the locations of the insects. The problem is to discover the highest concentration of a particular insect that should be controlled.

HYPOTHESIS

To fully form a hypothesis, it is necessary to select various locations that might be havens for the highest populations of a certain insect. For example, the highest concentration of roaches might be in the gymnasium, or the largest population of fruit flies might be in the cafeteria. Based on the answers to the research questions in this activity, write an educated guess concerning where you believe the insects are most abundant.

MATERIALS

- *for roaches, a glue trap or Roach Motel*
- *for flies, fly paper*
- *for ants, glue or other type of trap*
- *graph paper, the larger the squares, the better*

PROCEDURE

1. Make a rough map of the building being studied. Include the names of the various rooms and areas. For example, map the cafeteria, gym, wing A, locker room, etc.

2. Using graphing paper, convert the map into a grid with each square on the grid representing approximately 20 square feet.

3. Place the traps in as many of the grids as possible. Try to cover the whole building equally.

4. Number the trap sites on the grid map.

5. Check the traps at least twice a week and keep a running count of the number of insects captured at each trap site on the grid map. This running count should be recorded on the grid map for every numbered trap site.

6. Discard captured insects, if possible. This will facilitate the counting process.

7. Continue checking the traps and keeping a running count on the grid for three to four weeks.

8. Alert the administration, custodial staff, and cafeteria staff of traps which should remain undisturbed if the experiment location is a school or church.

9. Place signs by the traps so they will not be disturbed.

10. If any traps are lost, replace them as soon as possible.

RESULTS

1. Record the total number of insects collected at each trap site on the grid map.

2. Enlarge the grid map onto a piece of poster board. Use of an opaque projector or overhead projector will make this process easier. (Ask the teacher for assistance.)

3. Record the final total of insects found at each numbered trap site on the new grid map for display at the science fair. To make the final grid map more appealing and readily understandable to judges, teachers, and other observers, incorporate colors on the grid map. For example, the grids that had 22-25 roaches might be colored red, the grids with 18-21 might be colored orange, and the grids with 14-17 might be colored yellow. If colors are used, be certain to include a legend on the grid map.

CONCLUSION

Look at the grid to find the areas of your experiment location that contain the highest and lowest populations of the target insect.

As science fair participants look at the grid map, it will be possible for them to quickly discern the areas of high and low insect population at the experiment location, as well as the exact number of insects in any given grid of the experiment location.

Note to Experimenter:

If clear-cut results are not obtained from the experiment, then consider the following:

    a. Extend the experiment.
    b. Change the bait or trap and extend the experiment.
    c. Consider whether or not the weather is affecting your outcome.
    d. Consider the last time a professional exterminator treated the building.
    e. Consider how often the traps were checked.

"EGG"CITING OSMOSIS

Have you ever soaked in a bath for a long time and noticed what happens to your fingertips? Some people say that your fingers have shriveled up or *pruned*.

What really happens is that water passes through the skin. The skin is not shriveling, but instead, it is expanding. The expanded skin bunches up and wrinkles.

Another example of this phenomenon is that grocery stores have misters in the produce sections. To keep their fruits and vegetables from being limp, misters spray water at certain time intervals to keep the produce fresh and crisp. The water moves into the plant cells, making them more rigid.

But how did store owners discover how often to spray their produce? Scientists performed experiments like the one below to find out how rapidly the water is moving in and out of cells.

PROBLEM

The process of water moving across a membrane from a high concentration to a low concentration is called *osmosis*. By adding sugar, the concentration of water can be altered. Will different concentrations of sugar affect how quickly water moves across a membrane?

HYPOTHESIS

The hypothesis can be stated in either positive or negative terms. Different concentrations of sugar affect how quickly water moves across a membrane, or different concentrations of sugar do not affect how quickly water moves across a membrane.

MATERIALS
- eight raw, uncracked eggs
- vinegar
- eight glass jars
- corn syrup
- balance
- distilled water

PROCEDURE

To do this experiment, the shells must be removed from the eggs. To accomplish this, follow procedure 1.

1. Completely submerse a raw uncracked egg in vinegar for at least 24 hours or until the shell has dissolved. Follow this procedure for all eight eggs. Use these eggs for the experiment.

2. Record the weight of each egg on the chart provided. Be certain to keep the eggs separate so that the weights of the eggs will not be confused.

3. Label two jars "100% corn syrup solution." Fill each jar with corn syrup. Place an egg in each jar. Mark these jars 1 and 2.

4. Label two jars "50% corn syrup solution." Fill each jar with ½ part corn syrup and ½ part water, well mixed. Place an egg in each jar. Mark these jars 3 and 4.

5. Label two jars "25% corn syrup solution." Fill each jar with ¼ part corn syrup and ¾ part water, well mixed. Place an egg in each jar. Mark these jars 5 and 6.

6. Label two jars "distilled water" and then fill each jar. Place an egg in each jar. Mark these jars 7 and 8.

7. At 15-minute intervals, rinse each egg with warm water and gently dry it. Weigh and record the weight of each egg on the chart provided.

   Hint: Before placing each egg back into its solution, stir to keep sugar solutions well mixed.

8. Continue the experiment, weighing and recording for two hours.

RESULTS

Be certain that the weights are properly recorded on the chart provided.

CONCLUSION

Plot the averages from the chart on the line graph provided for this experiment. Be certain to color-code the legend on the graph with colored map pencils. Also, use the same colored map pencils that correspond with the legend to complete the graph.

By looking at the changing weight of the eggs on the graph, determine which sugar concentration prompted the most rapid movement of water across the membrane.

Look at the graph. Notice the weights of the eggs that were placed in sugar solutions. The eggs placed in the sugar solutions are decreasing in weight because there is more water inside the eggs than outside the eggs. Therefore, due to osmosis, the water moves out and the water decreases.

On the other hand, the eggs placed in distilled water are increasing in weight because there is more water outside the eggs than inside. Once again, osmosis is causing the movement of water.

UNSCRAMBLING THE EGGS

Time in Minutes

Egg Group	0	15	30	45	60	75	90	105	120
100%									
100%									
Average									
50%									
50%									
Average									
25%									
25%									
Average									
Distilled Water									
Distilled Water									
Average									

OSMOSIS GRAPH

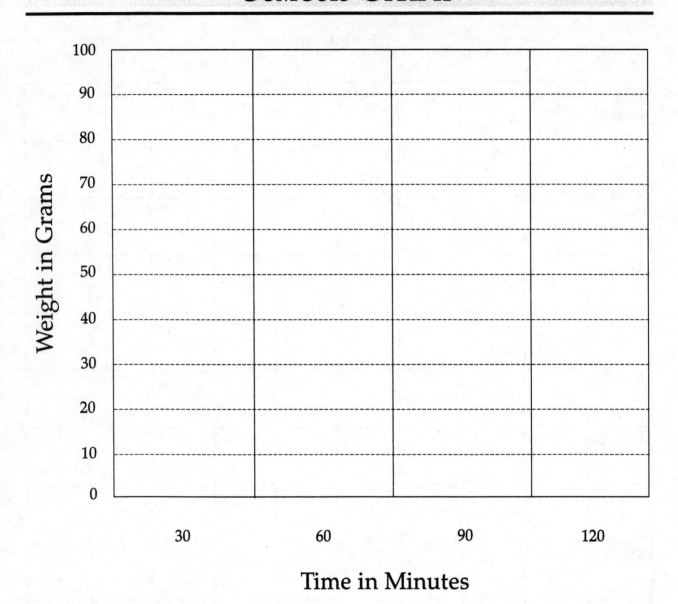

Weight in Grams

30   60   90   120

Time in Minutes

☐ 100% Syrup   ☐ 50% Syrup   ☐ 25% Syrup   ☐ 0% Syrup

RAINBOW CHEESE

You may remember from your younger years the tale of *Green Eggs and Ham* by Dr. Seuss. One of the characters in that story did not want to try green eggs and ham under any circumstances. Even though they most likely tasted the same as country eggs and ham, the perception of the food being green made it less appealing. Although the main character liked green eggs and ham at the end of the story, it is important to remember that people's perception of food often determines whether or not they will like it.

In the business world, advertisers are interested in food colors that will appeal to consumers. Blue M&M's came on the scene after the other colors had been introduced. But this occurred only after much research and experimentation and many taste tests.

One way food companies find out what people will buy is to run experiments called *taste tests*.

PROBLEM

Does the color of cream cheese affect people's perception of the taste?

HYPOTHESIS

The hypothesis can be stated in either positive or negative terms. The color of cream cheese affects people's perception of the taste. Conversely, the color of cream cheese does not affect people's perception of the taste.

MATERIALS

- red, blue, and green food color
- soft-spread cream cheese
- saltine crackers
- Dixie cups for water
- napkins
- pencils
- questionnaire for tasters (master copy provided)

PROCEDURE

1. Prepare four equal portions of soft-spread cream cheese. Color one red by mixing a few drops of red food color in softened cream cheese. Color one blue and another green in the same manner. Leave the final portion white. When these four portions are stored, keep them in an unmarked container so that the individuals in the taste test will not know that they are eating cream cheese, only that they are eating Rainbow Cheese.

2. Set up a booth at school for the taste test. (Check with administrators or building supervisors to determine the potential location and time for the booth. You may need to set up more than one day to get at least 100 tasters.)

3. Once the booth is set up, line up the different colors of cheese for the tasters. Have several sets ready so that more than one person can do the taste test at a time. Serve the cheese on saltine crackers.

4. Do not tell the tasters that they are eating cream cheese, only the new product, Rainbow Cheese.

5. Tasters must take a bit of plain saltine cracker in between each bite of Rainbow Cheese.

6. Keep water in a small Dixie cup available to tasters at all times.

7. Tasters must taste all four Rainbow Cheeses for their results to be used in the experiment.

8. Tasters must fill out the questionnaire provided, choosing their favorite Rainbow Cheese.

9. The experimenter must have at least 100 tasters in the taste test. The more tasters, the more accurate the results will be.

RESULTS

Tally the questionnaires to determine the favorite Rainbow Cheese. There should be a total for red, blue, green, and white. You should report the total number of individuals in the taste test on the bar graph, as well.

CONCLUSION

Complete the bar graph using the graphing sheet provided.

Using the bar graph, determine which Rainbow Cheese is the favorite. If there is no clear preference, then one could conclude that the color did not affect the tasters' perceptions of the food. On the other hand, if there is a clear preference, then color did affect the tasters' perceptions of food since the soft cream cheese tasted the same.

RAINBOW CHEESE QUESTIONNAIRE

Directions for tasters:

1. Do not put your name on this form.

2. You may participate in this taste test only once.

3. You must taste all four Rainbow Cheeses for your results to be tabulated.

4. Eat a bite of plain saltine cracker in between each bite of cheese to clear your palate.

5. Do not discuss Rainbow Cheeses with other tasters or make verbal comments about the cheeses during the taste test.

6. Drink water as needed during the taste test.

7. After you have tried all four Rainbow Cheeses, circle the cheese you prefer most on this form.

Circle One.

Red Rainbow Cheese

Blue Rainbow Cheese

Green Rainbow Cheese

White Rainbow Cheese

THANK YOU FOR YOUR PARTICIPATION IN THE RAINBOW CHEESE TASTE TEST!

YOUR SUPPORT IS APPRECIATED!

RAINBOW GRAPH

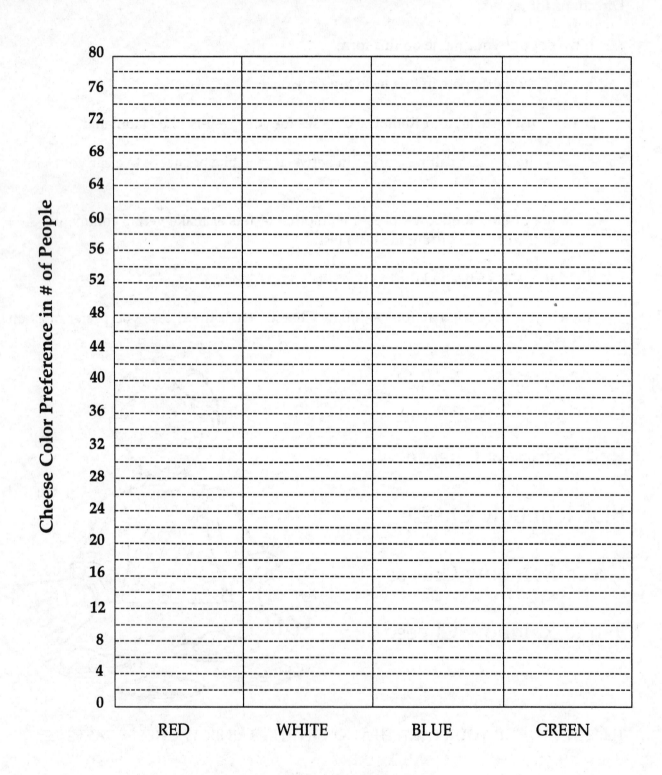

Cheese Color Preference in # of People

80
76
72
68
64
60
56
52
48
44
40
36
32
28
24
20
16
12
8
4
0

RED   WHITE   BLUE   GREEN

Color of Cheese

HEART ROCK

There are many different kinds of music. Music affects people's moods, which is why certain music is played during certain movie scenes. For instance, suspenseful music is played during a mystery, love songs are played in a romance, and action adventures have pulsating music. But does music simply add to the creation of a mood or does it actually affect a person's heart rate?

An experimenter can test the effect listening to certain kinds of music has on heart rate.

PROBLEM

Does music affect one's heart rate?

HYPOTHESIS

The hypothesis can be stated in either positive or negative terms. Music affects one's heart rate, or music does not affect one's heart rate.

MATERIALS

- tape player or CD player

- headphones

- stopwatch or a watch with a sweeping second hand

- music tape or CD with a driving beat, such as hard rock or rap

- music tape or CD with a soothing mellow beat, such as easy listening, new age, or soft love songs

PROCEDURE

To determine heart rate, it will be necessary to monitor the subject's pulse. There are two places recommended for monitoring the pulse. One is at the neck on the carotid artery on either side of the windpipe. The other is on the inside of the wrist beneath the thumb. When taking a subject's pulse, always use the first two fingers. Do not use the thumb to feel the pulse since there is a large artery in the thumb which may produce incorrect data. Be certain to practice monitoring the pulse on yourself as well as on another individual.

To determine heartbeats per minute, take the subject's pulse for 30 seconds, using a stopwatch or a watch with a sweeping second hand. Count each pulse during this time. Multiply this number by two. For example, if the pulse for 30 seconds is 35, then the number of heartbeats per minute is 70.

1. Select ten subjects.

2. Ask the subject to be seated and to get comfortable and remain relaxed for three or four minutes before beginning the test.

3. Take the subject's resting or normal heart rate and record it on the chart provided.

4. Place headphones on the subject and play music with a driving beat, such as hard rock or rap. Do not tell the subject what type of music he or she will hear. Use the same music selections for all subjects. Play the music at a volume level comfortable for the subject.

5. When seven minutes have passed, take the subject's pulse while the music continues to play.

6. Let the music continue to play for seven more minutes.

7. Take the subject's pulse a second time while the fast music is still playing. Record the results on the chart given.

8. Average the two pulse readings taken from the subject while he/she was listening to the first type of music. Record the average on the chart as well.

9. For the second part of the procedure, wait at least one day before testing with the second type of music. Be certain to use the same subjects.

10. Repeat procedures 2-8 using music with a soothing, mellow beat such as easy listening, new age, or soft love songs.

RESULTS

Complete the chart provided. Using the data from the chart, fill in the bar graph on the graph provided. Two copies of this graph will be needed. Be certain to follow the legend so that each subject has a bar for resting heart rate, fast-music heart rate, and slow-music heart rate.

CONCLUSION

When viewing the data and the bar graph, determine whether the subjects' heart rates were affected by music. Were they elevated during fast music or slowed during soothing music? Does one type of music affect the heart rate differently from the other?

HEART RATE CHART

Subject's Name	Resting Heart 1	Resting Heart 2	Resting Avg.	Fast Song 1	Fast Song 2	Fast Avg.	Slow Song 1	Slow Song 2	Slow Avg.

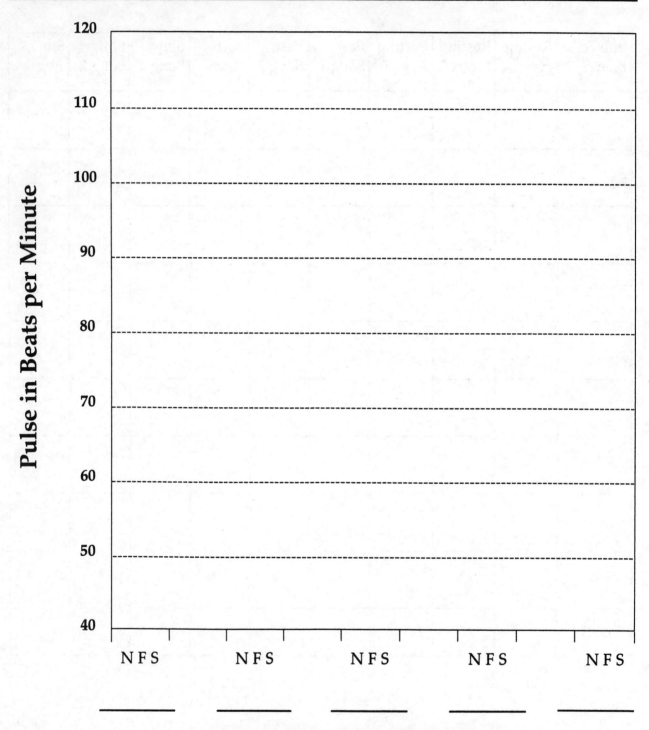

SUBJECTS' NAMES

N = Normal resting pulse rate
F = Pulse rate during fast music
S = Pulse rate during slow music

MUTANT RADISHES ON THE RAMPAGE

Science fiction has long been fascinated with the possibilities of mutation. Teenage Mutant Ninja Turtles, Killer Tomatoes, X-Men, and Spider Man are examples. Mutation is a change in the genetic makeup, that is, the DNA sequence, that can be passed on or inherited.

It is possible to purchase radish seeds that have been mutated. (See information from Carolina Biological in the materials section and in the back of the book on the resources page.) The seeds have been mutated by exposure to Cobalt 60 for varying lengths of time.

PROBLEM

What effects does exposure to Cobalt 60 have on radish seed germination?

HYPOTHESIS

The hypothesis can be stated in either positive or negative terms. Exposure to Cobalt 60 affects radish seed germination, or exposure to Cobalt 60 does not affect radish seed germination.

MATERIALS

- *potting soil*
- *radish seeds exposed to Cobalt 60 for varying lengths of time*
- *five aluminum pie plates (nine inch) for planting*

Radish seeds, which come in a kit and contain all five exposures to Cobalt 60, including seeds with no exposure, can be purchased for this experiment from:

Carolina Biological   Phone 1-800-334-5551
2700 York Road   FAX 1-800-222-7112
Burlington, N.C. 27215-3398

PROCEDURE

1. Order radish seeds from Carolina Biological. (Read the company's information and instructions about planting and care.)

2. Plant each group of seeds in a nine-inch pie plate that contains potting soil. Be certain that the seeds are equally distributed in the pie plate. Also, check to make certain that each pie plate has the same number of seeds planted.

3. Label each pie plate with the appropriate amount of exposure. There will be five pie plates in all.

4. Place pie plates in a sunny place and follow instructions for proper care.

5. Allow seeds to germinate for three weeks.

RESULTS

Use the enclosed journal page to record the date the seeds were planted and the number of seeds planted in each pie plate. Be certain to designate the level of exposure under "Radish Group." At the end of three weeks, count the number of seeds germinated in each pie plate and record on the journal page.

CONCLUSION

Observe the various pie plates as the seeds are germinating and at the end of three weeks. Check which pie plate contained the most germinated seeds and which one contained the fewest.

Use the attached grid for creating a bar graph to show how many seeds germinated for each of the different radish groups. Use different colored pencils for each bar on the bar graph.

Draw a conclusion about the effects of exposure to Cobalt 60 on radish seed germination.

Finally, look for interesting differences in the appearance of the seedlings as the exposure to Cobalt 60 increases.

RADISH RECORD KEEPING

Radish Group	Date Planted	Number of Seeds Planted	Number of Seeds Germinated	Date Completed

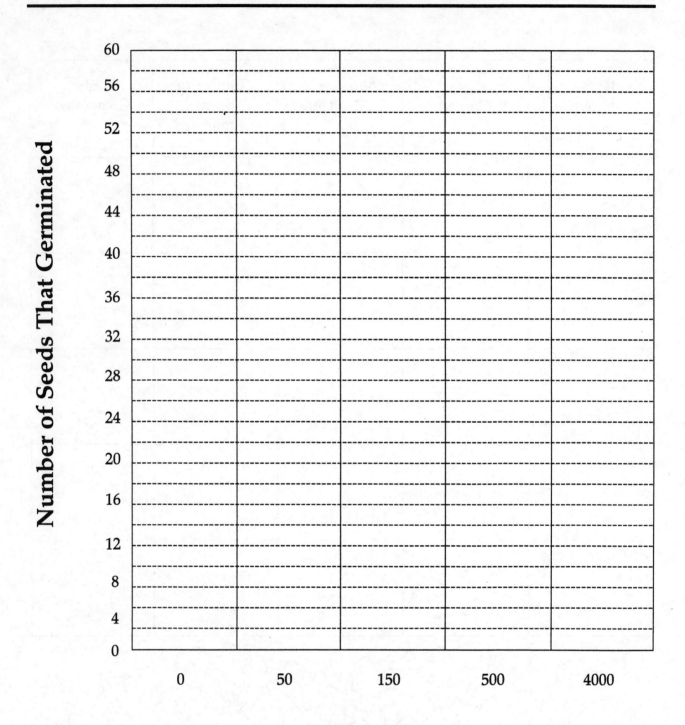

Number of Seeds That Germinated (y-axis: 0, 4, 8, 12, 16, 20, 24, 28, 32, 36, 40, 44, 48, 52, 56, 60)

Rads (x-axis: 0, 50, 150, 500, 4000)

PLANT NAP

All animals need sleep. Nocturnal animals, such as bats and owls, sleep during the day; their waking hours are at night. Diurnal animals, such as squirrels and birds, sleep at night.

Plants experience darkness and light as well. Plants respond to varying amounts of light. Thus, since there is more light in the summer, some plants bloom in the summer, while other plants bloom in the winter when the days are shorter. Additionally, greenhouses can grow seasonal plants year-round by tricking the plants into growing with more or less light.

PROBLEM

If plants grow bigger with more light, then will they grow even more with continuous light? Or do plants need sleep? Do plants require a period of darkness?

HYPOTHESIS

The hypothesis can be stated in either positive or negative terms. Plants need a period of darkness daily, or plants do not need a period of darkness daily.

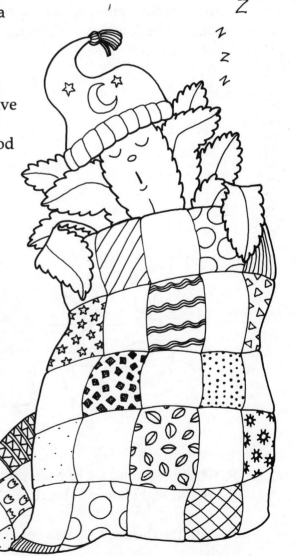

MATERIALS

- Dixie cups
- potting soil
- bean seeds
- aluminum pie plates
- two light timers
- three grow lights (can be purchased at Wal-Mart)
- lamps for the grow lights
- three dark rooms or closets
- metric ruler
- thermometer

PROCEDURE

1. Punch three holes in the bottoms of 12 Dixie cups to allow excess water to drain.

2. Fill each cup with potting soil.

3. Press two bean seeds into each cup one-half inch deep and then cover.

4. Place four Dixie cups on three different aluminum pie plates.

5. Select three dark areas and place aluminum pie plates in each area.

6. Fill a Dixie cup one-half full of water and pour this amount of water into each Dixie cup with bean seeds.

7. With the first set of bean seeds, arrange the grow lights to be on for eight hours and off for 16 hours a day. Use a timer to automatically regulate the light. Take care that the lights are not too close to the plants or the heat could damage the plants. Check with your parents or teachers to make certain that the lights are not a fire hazard.

8. With the second set of bean seeds, arrange the grow lights to be on 16 hours and off eight hours a day. Use a timer to automatically regulate the light.

9. With the third set of bean seeds, arrange the grow lights to be on 24 hours a day.

10. Water the plants with the same amount of water, a half Dixie cup, every three days.

11. At the time of watering, measure each plant's height by placing a metric ruler on the top of the soil next to the plant. Record the height in centimeters on the chart provided. (Note: Two seeds were planted in each Dixie cup to ensure germination. However, only one measurement will be taken for each cup. Therefore, if two plants sprout in one cup, simply clip the smaller one.)

12. Average the height of each set of four plants each time they are measured. Record the averages on the chart provided.

13. Continue the experiment for one month.

14. Check the temperature of all locations periodically to see whether they are similar.

RESULTS

Create a graph by plotting the average plant height for each set of four plants at each site. Be certain to include a legend which designates a different color for each plant set.

CONCLUSION

Look at the graph to determine under which lighting circumstances the plants thrive best. Do plants require a period of darkness? What happened to the plants under continuous light? What about the plants with only eight hours of light? Report the general appearance of the plants. For instance, report leaf size, yellowing, and overall health.

PLANT NAP CHART

Plant Group A	Day 0	Day 3	Day 6	Day 9	Day 12	Day 15	Day 18	Day 21	Day 24	Day 27	Day 30
Plant 1											
Plant 2											
Plant 3											
Plant 4											
Average											
Plant Group B											
Plant 1											
Plant 2											
Plant 3											
Plant 4											
Average											
Plant Group C											
Plant 1											
Plant 2											
Plant 3											
Plant 4											
Average											

NAPPING PLANT GRAPH

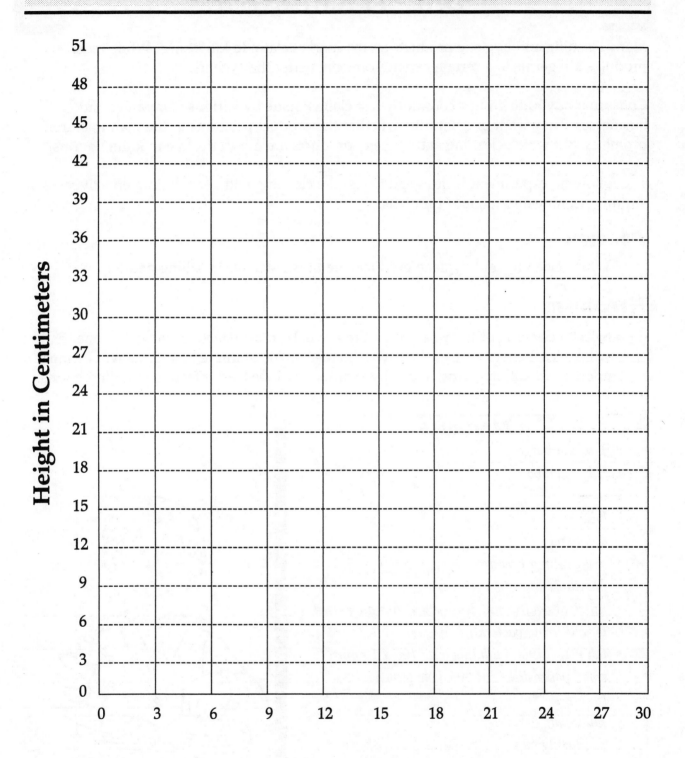

Time in Days

BAC-TERMINATOR

Many cleaning and hygiene products on the market claim to kill germs. While most products kill germs to a certain extent, some are better than others.

Consumer advocate groups constantly test claims made by various companies and businesses. They want to determine whether the product performs as the manufacturer promises. But which cleaning and hygiene products are most effective in killing germs?

The following experiment is designed to test the cleaning and germ-killing effectiveness of various cleaning and hygiene products.

PROBLEM

Which cleaning and hygiene products are most effective in killing germs?

HYPOTHESIS

Select a cleaning or hygiene product that will be most effective, as well as one that will be least effective. Develop two statements. For example, ammonia will be most effective in killing germs, and baby shampoo will be least effective in killing germs.

MATERIALS

- raw hamburger
- baby shampoo
- water
- bleach
- ammonia
- dishwashing liquid
- mouthwash
- nutrient agar (a nutritive jelled substance used for culturing bacteria)
- ten petri dishes with lids (size 100 x 15 mm)
- small paper disks cut by a hole punch
- tweezers
- sauce pan
- measuring cup
- metric ruler
- paper towel
- rubber gloves

PROCEDURE

1. Prepare the dehydrated nutrient agar in a sauce pan using medium-low heat. Follow the directions on the container. However, divide all measurements by four since you will not need the full recipe.

If nutrient agar is not readily available through the school's science program, it can easily be ordered from: NASCO (two locations) 1-800-558-9595

901 Janesville Avenue	4825 Stoddard Road
Fort Atkinson, Wisconsin	Modesto, California
zip 53538-0901	zip 95356-9318
ph. 414-563-2446	ph. 209-545-1600
FAX 414-563-8296	FAX 209-545-1669

2. Once the nutrient agar is prepared, pour it into ten petri dishes. It is most easily dispensed from a small measuring cup. Pour enough agar so that it just covers the bottom of each petri dish. Cover it with the lid and allow the agar to gel. The agar will solidify quickly when it reaches room temperature. Check with your teacher to see whether the school can loan petri dishes. If not, sterile disposable petri dishes can be ordered from:

WARDS BIOLOGY SUPPLIES
P.O. Box 92912
Rochester, New York 14692-9012
ph. 1-800-962-2660
FAX 1-800-635-8431

3. Store the solidified agar petri dishes in the refrigerator until they are needed.

4. Allow thawed hamburger to sit at room temperature for three hours.

5. Wearing a pair of rubber gloves, pinch a piece of hamburger and gently blot the full surface of the agar evenly on each petri dish. For each petri dish, get a new pinch of hamburger.

6. Using a hole punch, punch out at least 60 small disks of paper. With a pencil, label ten disks "A," ten disks "B," through ten disks labeled "F." Each letter will represent a cleaning or hygiene product.

7. Soak the ten disks marked "A" in bleach. Remove the paper disks with a pair of tweezers and touch the disks gently on a dry paper towel to blot excess fluid. Place one disk in each of the ten petri dishes, locating each disk five millimeters from the side of the dish at the twelve o'clock position.

8. Soak the ten disks marked "B" in ammonia. Remove the paper disks with a pair of tweezers and touch the disks gently on a dry paper towel to blot excess fluid. Place one disk in each of the ten petri dishes, locating each disk five millimeters from the side of the dish at the two o'clock position.

9. Soak the ten disks marked "C" in dishwashing liquid. Remove the paper disks with a pair of tweezers and touch the disks gently on a dry paper towel to blot excess fluid. Place one disk in each of the ten petri dishes, locating each disk five millimeters from the side of the dish at the four o'clock position.

10. Soak the ten disks marked "D" in baby shampoo. Remove the paper disks with a pair of tweezers and touch the disks gently on a dry paper towel to blot excess fluid. Place one disk in each of the ten petri dishes, locating each disk five millimeters from the side of the dish at the six o'clock position.

11. Soak the ten disks marked "E" in mouthwash. Remove the paper disks with a pair of tweezers and touch the disks gently on a dry paper towel to blot excess fluid. Place one disk in each of the ten petri dishes, locating each disk five millimeters from the side of the dish at the eight o'clock position.

12. Soak the ten disks marked "F" in water. Remove the paper disks with a pair of tweezers and touch the disks gently on a dry paper towel to blot excess fluid. Place one disk in each of the ten petri dishes, locating each disk five millimeters from the side of the dish at the ten o'clock position.

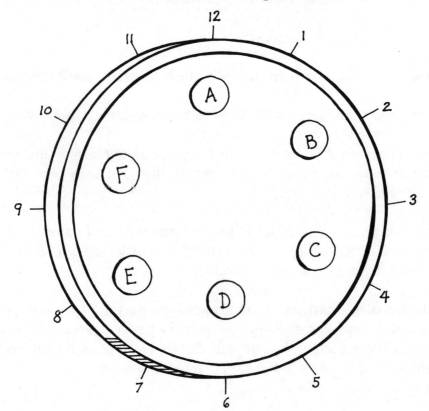

13. Place the petri dishes in a dark warm place for 36 hours. The bacteria should be grown over the agar plate except around the disks. The area clear of bacteria with no growth is the "zone of inhibition." The size of this zone of inhibition corresponds to the effectiveness of the product.

14. Using a metric ruler, measure the radius of each of the clear areas. Begin at the center of the disk and measure to the closest area where bacteria begins. Record the values on the chart provided.

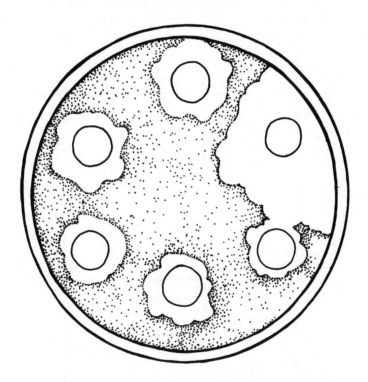

RESULTS

Using the completed chart, average the ten measurements taken for each cleaning or hygiene product. Plot the average measurements for each product on the bar graph sheet provided.

CONCLUSION

Review the bar graph, as well as the formulated hypotheses. The product with the largest measurement was the most effective, while the product with the smallest measurement was the least effective. Report the accuracy of the stated hypotheses. Does it seem that the manufacturers' claims hold up when the products are tested?

ZONE OF INHIBITION

measured in millimeters

Product Name	Dish 1	Dish 2	Dish 3	Dish 4	Dish 5	Dish 6	Dish 7	Dish 8	Dish 9	Dish 10	Avg.
Bleach											
Water											
Mouthwash											
Dishwashing Liquid											
Ammonia											
Baby Shampoo											

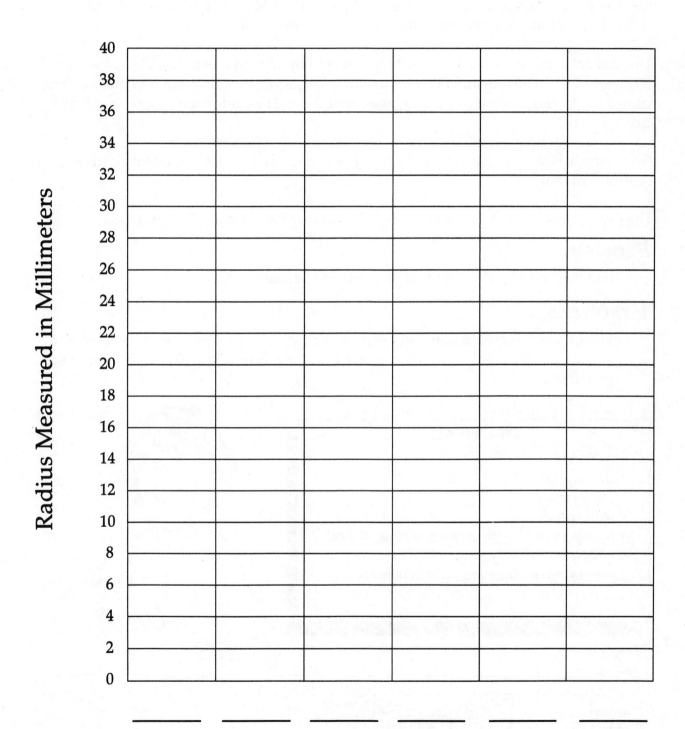

Radius Measured in Millimeters

Products

ACID RAIN

Environmental groups have warned against problems related to acid rain. They have called for a reduction in the amount of acid rain. But how much of a problem is it?

The main cause of acid rain is air pollution caused by cars and factories. The fumes they release mix with the rain and fall back to earth. The acidic nature of the rain builds up in lakes and streams, affecting living organisms in them. The acid rain also affects soil and crops.

Great efforts have gone into controlling and reducing car exhaust and factory emissions to control acid rain.

The experiment below is designed to test the effects of acid on seed germination.

PROBLEM

Will increased levels of acid affect bean seed germination?

HYPOTHESIS

The hypothesis can be stated in positive or negative terms. Increased levels of acid will affect bean seed germination or increased levels of acid will not affect bean seed germination.

MATERIALS

- *bean seeds*
- *eleven pint jars*
- *Dixie cups*
- *potting soil*
- *ninety-grain vinegar (pickling vinegar at local grocery)*
- *measuring cup (that measures in ounces)*

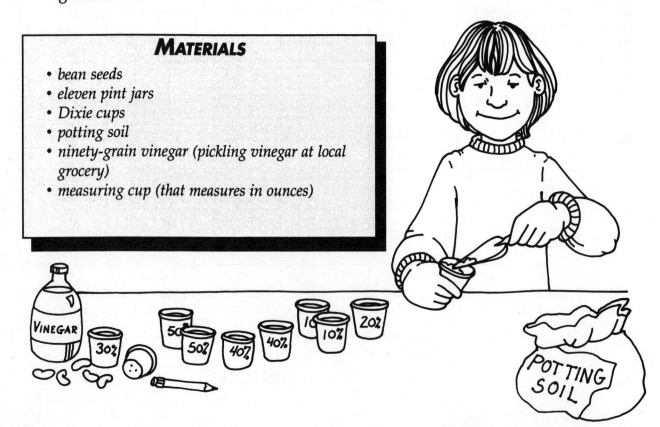

PROCEDURE

1. Mix the following amounts of vinegar and water and label each jar with the amount of acid in ten percent gradations

   a. 10 ounces of 90 grain vinegar (100%)
   b. 9 ounces of 90 grain vinegar and 1 ounce of water (90%)
   c. 8 ounces of 90 grain vinegar and 2 ounces of water (80%)
   d. 7 ounces of 90 grain vinegar and 3 ounces of water (70%)
   e. 6 ounces of 90 grain vinegar and 4 ounces of water (60%)
   f. 5 ounces of 90 grain vinegar and 5 ounces of water (50%)
   g. 4 ounces of 90 grain vinegar and 6 ounces of water (40%)
   h. 3 ounces of 90 grain vinegar and 7 ounces of water (30%)
   i. 2 ounces of 90 grain vinegar and 8 ounces of water (20%)
   j. 1 ounce of 90 grain vinegar and 9 ounces of water (10%)
   k. 10 ounces of water (0%).

2. Place ten bean seeds in each pint jar and allow them to soak for 24 hours.

3. Poke holes in the bottoms of 22 Dixie cups and fill with potting soil. Label two cups for each varying level of vinegar and water by percents. For example, two cups labeled "100%," two cups labeled "90%," two cups labeled "80%," all the way down to two cups labeled "0%."

4. Remove the ten bean seeds from the jar. Blot dry. Place five bean seeds in one of the Dixie cups marked with the correct percent and five bean seeds in the other marked Dixie cup.

5. Place one-half inch of potting soil over the bean seeds.

6. Repeat this for all 11 pint jars. There will be a total of 22 Dixie cups with five beans in each cup.

7. Place all the Dixie cups in a sunny area.

8. Water with a half Dixie cup every three days.

9. Continue the experiment for two weeks.

10. At the intervals designated on the chart provided, record the data by counting the number of beans sprouted.

Results

On the last day, data is collected by counting all the beans sprouted. Use that total to develop a bar graph using the sheet provided.

Conclusion

Consider whether the higher levels of acid affected bean seed germination by viewing the chart and graph. Determine whether the stated hypothesis is correct.

ACIDIC SEED SPROUTING

Record the total number of seeds that have sprouted on each of the days indicated.

Percent Vinegar	2 Days	4 Days	6 Days	8 Days	10 Days	12 Days	14 Days Total
100%							
90%							
80%							
70%							
60%							
50%							
40%							
30%							
20%							
10%							
0%							

ACIDIC SEED GERMINATION GRAPH

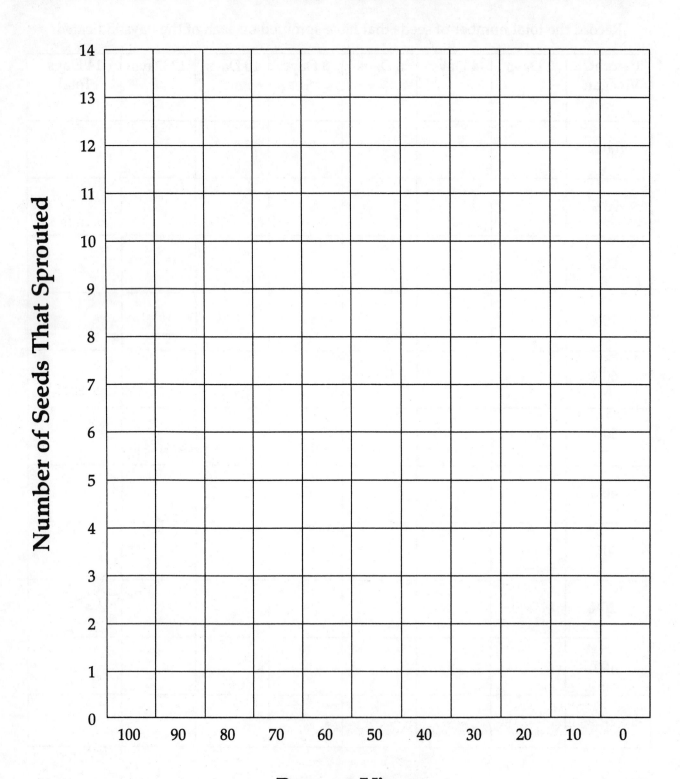

Number of Seeds That Sprouted (y-axis)

Percent Vinegar (x-axis)

TONS-O-TRASH

According to the Environmental Defense Fund, the average American generates three and a half pounds of garbage a day. This includes garbage from school, work, home, or around town. This comes to a total of a half ton of garbage per year for every American. In a lifetime this could be as much as 45 tons of garbage per American.

It would be interesting to see how much garbage five families produce at home each week. The following experiment is designed to find the answer.

Many people believe that some disposables can be reused or recycled. For example, aluminum, glass, paper, and plastic recycling can reduce the amount of garbage thrown away. The first step, however, in reducing garbage amounts is to realize how much is thrown away.

PROBLEM

How much trash is produced by the people in five families in a week?

HYPOTHESIS

Using the information in the introduction, estimate the amount of trash that each person in a family will generate in a week.

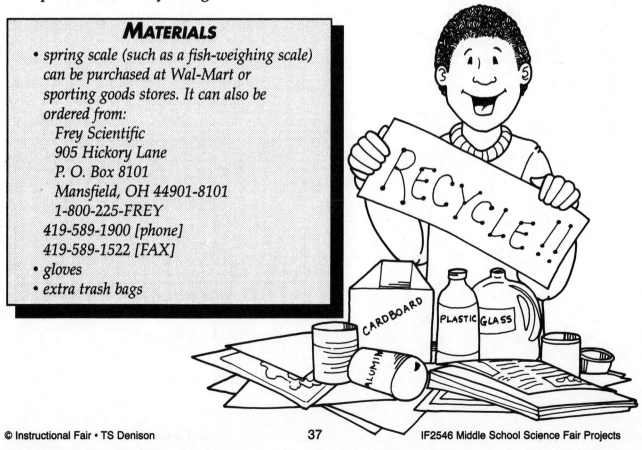

MATERIALS
- *spring scale (such as a fish-weighing scale) can be purchased at Wal-Mart or sporting goods stores. It can also be ordered from:*
    Frey Scientific
    905 Hickory Lane
    P. O. Box 8101
    Mansfield, OH 44901-8101
    1-800-225-FREY
    419-589-1900 [phone]
    419-589-1522 [FAX]
- *gloves*
- *extra trash bags*

PROCEDURE

1. Request that four neighboring families allow you to weigh the garbage they dispose of for three weeks along with your own family's garbage.

2. Tell each family to continue to throw things away as usual and not to attempt to increase or decrease the amount of trash for the duration of the experiment.

3. Ask each family to place the trash in a trash bag so that it can be weighed most efficiently.

4. Most garbage is collected curb-side twice a week in a neighborhood. In this case, weigh the garbage the night before collection or the morning of the collection, depending on when the neighbors set out their garbage.

5. If your neighbors live in apartments, volunteer to take their garbage to the dumpster every two or three days. This will allow you a chance to weigh it and help your neighbors at the same time.

6. To weigh the garbage, hook the spring scale or fish scale to the bag and lift it.

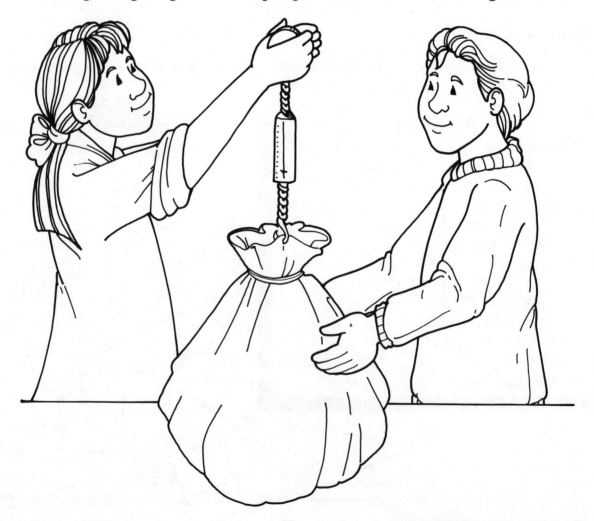

7. Record the weight of the garbage on the chart provided.

8. If the bag weighs more than what can be measured by the scale, then place some of the garbage in an extra trash bag. Weigh the two lighter bags instead of one heavy one. Be certain to use gloves to move any garbage from one bag to another.

9. Continue this experiment for three weeks.

10. At the end of the experiment, circulate the questionnaire provided. This information may be helpful when drawing conclusions.

RESULTS

Look at the chart and calculate the average weekly weight of garbage for each family. Record the averages on the chart.

Since some families are larger than others, divide the average weekly garbage weight by the number of people in that family. This will tell how much garbage each person in that family is generating. Record this number on the chart as well.

CONCLUSION

Look at the completed chart and consider the hypothesis. Are families producing more or less garbage than you expected?

Examine the completed questionnaires and determine why some families may be producing more or less garbage than others.

TALKING TRASH

A Questionnaire About Recycling

1. Does your family recycle? (circle one) YES   NO

2. If yes, please circle the types of items that your family recycles.

   aluminum   glass

   tin cans   newspaper

   plastic   oil/oil filters

   cardboard   paper other than newspaper

   other (please list) _____

3. Does your family compost? (circle one) YES   NO

4. If yes, please circle the types of material that your family composts.

   grass clippings   leaves

   organic kitchen scraps   paper

   other (please list) _____

5. Does your family purchase refills at the grocery store to reduce packaging waste?
   (circle one) YES   NO

6. Would your family consider buying more of these products if they were available?
   (circle one) YES   NO

7. Could your family reduce its weekly amount of trash? (circle one) YES   NO
   Briefly explain: _____

   _____

   _____

HEAVYWEIGHT TRASH CHART

Family Names	Week 1 Weight (in lbs.)	Week 2 Weight (in lbs.)	Week 3 Weight (in lbs.)	Average Weekly Weight (in lbs.)	Number of People in Family	Weight of Trash Made by Each Person

TALKING TO PLANTS

For years herbalists and plant lovers have claimed that talking to their plants helps to enhance the plants' growth and overall health. Is there a logical explanation for such a claim?

When people talk and exhale they are giving off carbon dioxide (CO_2). Carbon dioxide is essential for healthy growth in plants. Will extra CO_2 help plants grow stronger and healthier?

PROBLEM

Does the growth and health of a plant increase with an additional amount of CO_2?

HYPOTHESIS

Hypothesis can be stated in either positive or negative terms. An additional amount of CO_2 increases plants' growth and health, or an additional amount of CO_2 does not affect plants' growth and health.

MATERIALS
- radish seeds
- Dixie cups
- potting soil
- two aquariums
- vinegar
- baking soda
- triple beam balance
- plastic wrap
- pint jar

PROCEDURE

1. Punch three small holes in the bottoms of eight Dixie cups to allow for excess water drainage.

2. Fill each cup with potting soil.

3. Place three radish seeds in each Dixie cup. Be certain to spread the seeds out and gently press them in about one-quarter inch and cover them with soil.

4. Place four plants in one aquarium which has been marked "carbon dioxide" and four plants in the other aquarium. The two aquariums should be placed close together.

5. Fill a Dixie cup half full of water. Gently water each cup with this amount of water.

6. Once each cup has been watered and drained for five minutes, each cup must be weighed. Remember to always weigh the plants after they have been watered and drained for five minutes. This will prevent the error of wet soil versus dry soil, which would affect the weight of the plant.

7. Record the weight of the plant on the chart given in the "Results" section.

8. One aquarium must have a higher concentration of CO_2 than the other. To acquire an additional amount of CO_2, place three tablespoons of baking soda in a pint jar. Next, add ⅓ cup vinegar and quickly set the jar inside the aquarium. When baking soda ($NaCO_3$) reacts with the vinegar, it releases CO_2.

9. Use the plastic wrap to partially cover the CO_2 aquarium, as well as the other aquarium. Both aquariums should have the same partial covering. The partial covering will prevent the escape of additional CO_2 added to the aquarium.

10. Replenish the CO_2 every morning and every evening. Be certain to rinse the pint jar before replenishing.

11. Weigh each plant once a week. Always remember to water the plants with equal amounts of water (half-full Dixie cup) and allow to drain five minutes prior to weighing. Record the weight on the chart provided.

12. Continue the experiment for five weeks.

13. Average the weekly weights of the four plants in the carbon dioxide aquarium as well as the weights of the four plants in the other aquarium. Record the averages on the chart provided.

RESULTS

After recording the weekly weights and averages of the plants on the chart, use the graph provided to plot the averages in a line graph. Be certain to use a legend to distinguish the two plant groups. Using two different colors helps to distinguish the two lines.

CONCLUSION

Examine the results of the experiment by looking at the line graph. Do obvious advantages exist in the group of plants that received additional CO_2? Do obvious disadvantages exist in those which did not? Does additional CO_2 promote plant growth and health?

PLANT CHAT CHART

CO₂ Plant Group	Day 0	Day 7	Day 14	Day 21	Day 28	Day 35
Plant 1						
Plant 2						
Plant 3						
Plant 4						
Average						
Plant Group Without CO₂						
Plant 1						
Plant 2						
Plant 3						
Plant 4						
Average						

PLANT GROWTH GRAPH

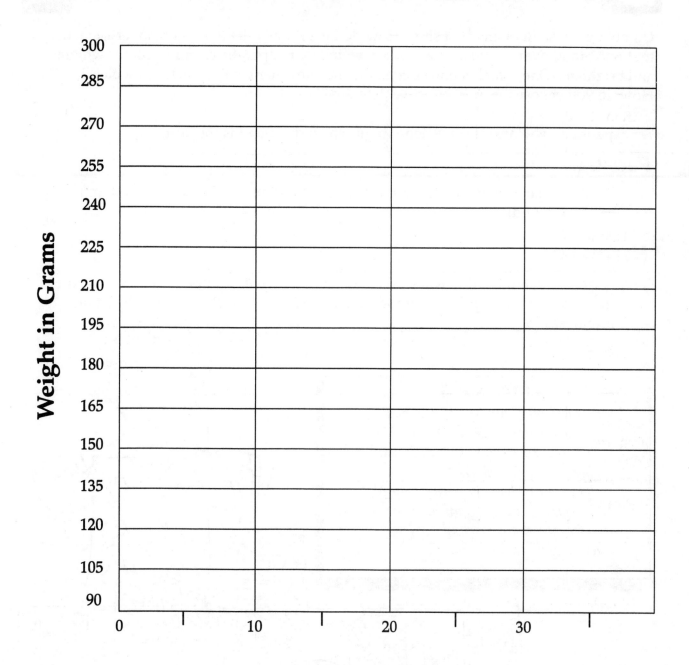

Time in Days

Draw a line beside each of the labels below showing the color you chose to use on the graph.

CO$_2$ Plants	Regular Plants

DETERGENT DILEMMA

Oh no! I got a stain on my best shirt! How do I get it out? The television advertisements tout one brand over another. One works well in any temperature, and the other whitens and brightens. One contains power crystals, and the other contains color-safe bleach. How do you choose the most effective detergent?

An experiment will answer questions about which detergent is the best.

PROBLEM

What is the best detergent for removing stains and producing the cleanest and brightest laundry?

HYPOTHESIS

Select the detergent that will be the most effective. For example, Cheer will be the most effective detergent for removing stains and leaving clothes the whitest and brightest.

MATERIALS

- four different laundry detergents. For example: Cheer, Tide, Wisk, and All.
- four pieces of white cotton cloth, such as pillow cases or T-shirts.
- eight stains: chocolate syrup, canned blueberries, red fruit punch, motor oil, ink, coffee, grass, and ketchup.
- washing machine

PROCEDURE

1. Stain the pieces of cloth with all the stains recommended. Be certain that you place each type of stain in the same place on each of the four pieces of cloth and use the same amount of stain each time. Use a consistent pattern when creating the stained pieces of cloth. Keep a record of where each stain is located. It is also a good idea to place a red or black stain in the upper left-hand corner of the cloth to help you locate the stains after washing.

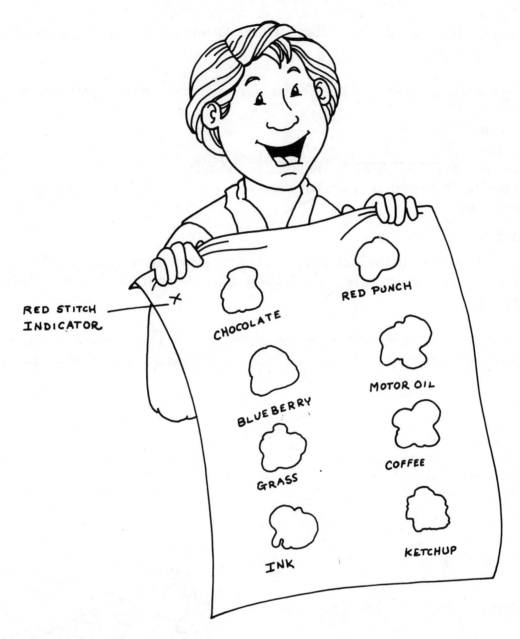

RED STITCH INDICATOR

CHOCOLATE

RED PUNCH

BLUEBERRY

MOTOR OIL

GRASS

COFFEE

INK

KETCHUP

2. Let the stains set for 24 hours.

3. Select the first detergent to be used for this experiment. Wash one of the stained pieces of fabric. Remember to use the exact amount of detergent called for in the directions. Some detergents may be concentrated, while others are not.

4. Repeat the same procedure for the other three stained cloths and laundry detergents. Be certain to always use the same temperature setting and wash cycle so that all detergents and stained cloths are tested similarly. All four stained cloths should be dried in the same way as well.

RESULTS

Look carefully at the stains on all four cloths. Determine the detergent that cleans the best and brightest.

Using the following scale, rate each stain for a specific detergent on the sheet provided.
  5 = completely clean
  4 = almost clean, can barely see stain
  3 = somewhat clean, stain clearly faded but visible
  2 = barely clean, stain only slightly removed
  1 = not clean

CONCLUSION

Tally the total score of the individual stains for a given detergent. Place the sum for each detergent in the score box. The highest score will indicate the best overall detergent.

Plot the scores of the individual detergents on the graph provided. View the graph to determine both the most effective and least effective detergents for removing stains.

SCORING STAINS

Stains	Detergent 1 _____	Detergent 2 _____	Detergent 3 _____	Detergent 4 _____
Chocolate				
Blueberry				
Grass				
Ink				
Red Punch				
Motor Oil				
Coffee				
Ketchup				
Overall Score				

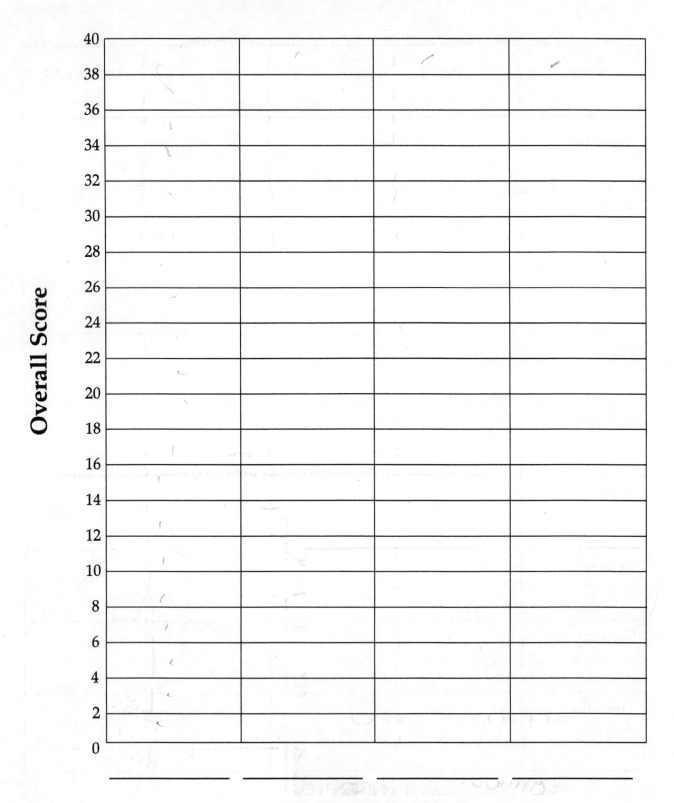

Detergents Used

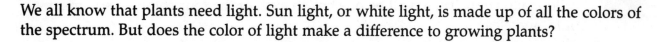

We all know that plants need light. Sun light, or white light, is made up of all the colors of the spectrum. But does the color of light make a difference to growing plants?

When we look at a colored object, we see the color that the object is reflecting, not the color the object is absorbing. For example, when looking at a red apple, we see red because the apple is reflecting red, not absorbing it.

When we look at plants, most of which are green, the plants are reflecting green light rather than absorbing and using it. Would plants thrive if their light source was green?

The experiment below tests the color preferences of light for tomato plants.

PROBLEM

Do plants prefer a certain color of light?

HYPOTHESIS

Hypotheses can be stated in positive or negative terms. For example, yes, plants prefer a certain color of light. Or, no, plants do not prefer a certain color of light.

MATERIALS

- *four large cardboard boxes*
- *measuring cup*
- *potting soil*
- *eight small tomato plants (approximately the same size) from a nursery*
- *aluminum pie plates*
- *metric ruler*
- *four different colors of cellophane (plastic wrap): red, green, blue, and clear*

PROCEDURE

1. Cut off the tops of the large cardboard boxes. Then cut large windows in all four sides of each box. Cover the tops and windows of the boxes with colored cellophane wrap. There will be one box in each of the four colors—red, green, blue, and clear.

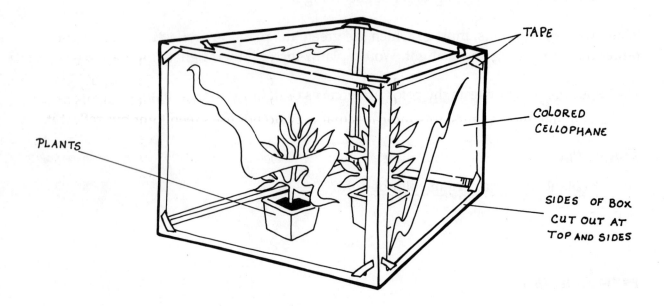

TAPE

COLORED CELLOPHANE

PLANTS

SIDES OF BOX CUT OUT AT TOP AND SIDES

2. Label the tomato plants this way: two plants red, two green, two blue, and two clear.

3. Measure each plant's height by placing the end of the metric ruler on the soil and recording the height in centimeters on the chart provided.

4. Place two plants, appropriately labeled, in each box.

5. Place all four boxes in a sunny area. Outside would be best.

6. Every three days, water each plant with one-half cup of water. Then measure the heights of the plants and record on the chart.

7. Continue the experiment for three weeks.

RESULTS

Examine the heights of the tomato plants recorded on the chart. Average the heights of the two tomato plants in each box for every three-day period of measurement. Do this for each group of plants that grew under the various colors of light. Once the averages are determined, plot the averages on the line graph provided. Be certain the color used on the line graph corresponds to the color of light used in the experiment. For example, use a red line to represent the growth of tomato plants in the box covered with red cellophane. To represent the clear cellophane, use a black line.

CONCLUSION

Inspect the line graphs. Notice the plants that gained the most height over the three-day period. They were receiving the most preferred light. Remember that objects reflect the color of light that they do not absorb or utilize. Since tomato plants are green, like most plants, this indicates that they do not use green light but reflect it. Sunlight, which is white light, contains all of the colors in the visible spectrum. The tomato plants in the clear plastic box may have been the most hardy, since they were receiving all the colors of the spectrum. However, does the graph reveal that tomato plants prefer one color of light over another?

SPECIAL SPECTRUM CHART

Record the height of each plant in centimeters.

Cellophane Color	Day 0	Day 3	Day 6	Day 9	Day 12	Day 15	Day 18	Day 21
Red - #1								
Red - #2								
Average								
Blue - #1								
Blue - #2								
Average								
Green - #1								
Green - #2								
Average								
Clear - #1								
Clear - #2								
Average								

Do Plants Have a Color Preference?

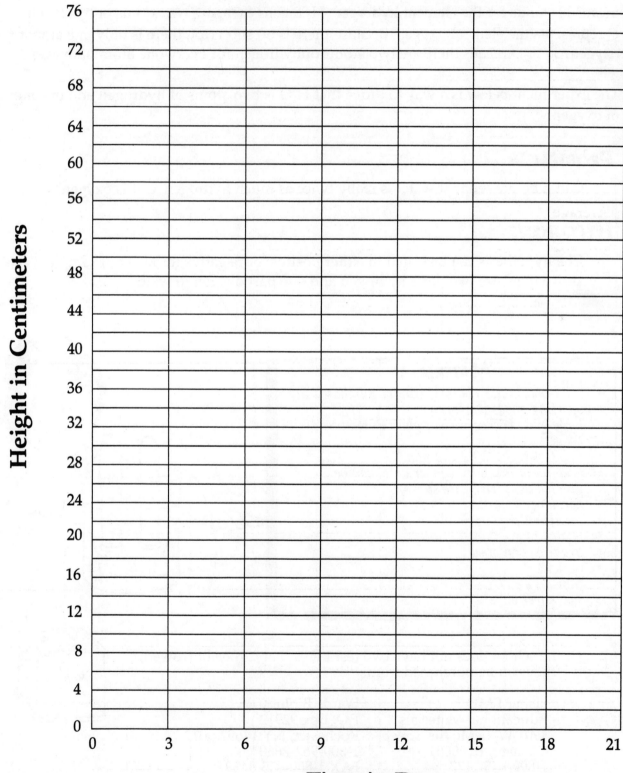

Height in Centimeters

Time in Days

PARTING THE WATERS

Water can also be written H_2O. Most people are familiar with H_2O, but what does it really mean? H stands for the element hydrogen. H_2 means there are two atoms of hydrogen. O represents the element oxygen. Because there is no subscript, there is only one atom of oxygen. So H_2O means there are two atoms of hydrogen for every one atom of oxygen.

The experiment below is a way to prove that H_2O is two atoms of hydrogen and one atom of oxygen.

PROBLEM

Can it be proved that water is really twice as much hydrogen as it is oxygen?

HYPOTHESIS

The hypothesis can be stated in either positive or negative terms. For example, I can prove there are two parts hydrogen and one part oxygen in water.

MATERIALS
- *a six-volt lantern battery (can be purchased in sporting goods stores)*
- *large glass beaker or clear glass Pyrex bread baker*
- *two test tubes, 20 x 150 mm.**
- *two feet of insulated copper wire (can be purchased at hardware stores)*
- *permanent marker*
- *metric ruler*
- *Scotch tape*
- *one teaspoon of salt*
- *camera*
- *film*
- *two paper clips*

*If the school does not have two test tubes that can be borrowed, they can be purchased from:

Fisher EMD
Educational Materials
4901 W. LeMoyne Street
Chicago, IL 60651
1-800-955-1177
FAX 312-378-7174

Wards Biology
P.O. Box 92912
Rochester, NY 14692-9012
1-800-962-2660
FAX 1-800-635-8439

PROCEDURE

1. Using a permanent marker and a metric ruler, begin from the bottom of the test tube and mark off eight centimeters. Mark one test tube positive and the other test tube negative.

2. Twist one end of a paper clip 90 degrees, so that the paper clip now has a hook. Tape the flat side of the paper clip halfway down the test tube with the Scotch tape. Do the same thing with the other test tube.

3. Fill the large glass beaker or Pyrex bread baker two-thirds full of water.

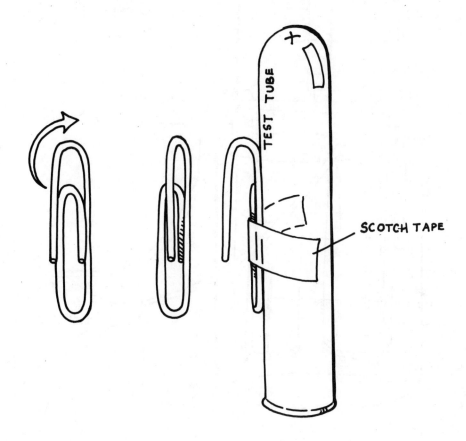

4. Fill both test tubes with water and then use the paper clip hooks to hang them on the sides of the glass beaker or Pyrex bread baker. The test tubes should be open side down. Be certain that there are no air bubbles in the test tubes. Half of each test tube should be out of the water.

5. Two lengths of insulated copper wire are needed, one foot each. Remove one inch of insulation off both ends of the two pieces of wire.

6. Connect one end of wire on the positive terminal of the battery. Bend the other end of the wire up into the test tube marked "positive."

7. Connect one end of the second length of wire on the negative terminal of the battery. Bend the other end of the wire up into the test tube marked "negative."

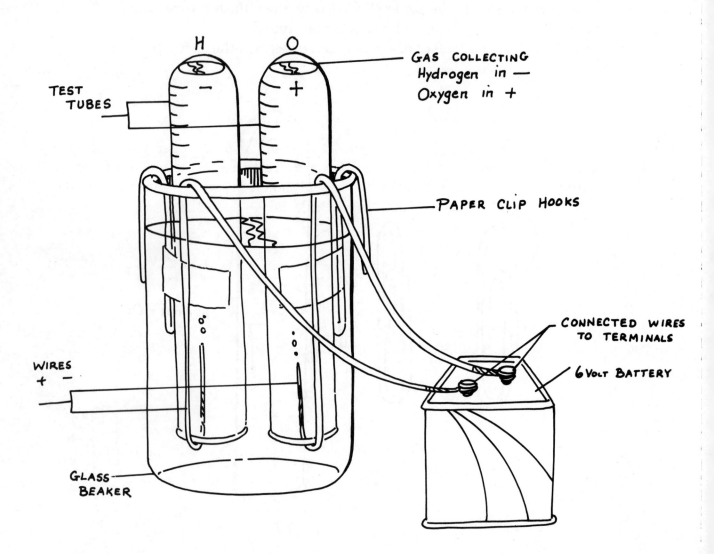

8. When the two wires are attached, bubbles should begin to form around the exposed wire. The test tubes will capture the gas being released.

9. Record the amount of gas collected in each test tube every two hours on the chart provided. Use the increments marked on the test tube to gauge the amount of gas being collected.

10. Take photos of the test tubes every two hours. The photographs will be glued to poster board and used in your presentation and display.

RESULTS

The bubbles forming around the wires are caused by the water being split into hydrogen atoms and oxygen atoms. The hydrogen atoms will gather around the exposed wire in the negative test tube. The oxygen atoms will gather around the exposed wire in the positive test tube. Notice that the negative test tube collected more gas than the positive.

Using the results recorded on the chart, construct a bar graph on the sheet provided. Color-code the bar graph by using red for hydrogen and blue for oxygen.

CONCLUSION

Consider the chart and graph and notice the amounts of hydrogen gas in comparison with the amounts of oxygen gas. To prove that water really is made up of two hydrogen atoms and one oxygen atom, there should be twice as much gas in the negative test tube (hydrogen) as there is in the positive test tube (oxygen).

SHOCKING WATER CHART

Time Intervals	Positive Test Tube	Negative Test Tube
2 hours		
4 hours		
6 hours		
8 hours		
10 hours		
12 hours		
14 hours		
16 hours		

HOW HIGH IS THE HYDROGEN GRAPH?

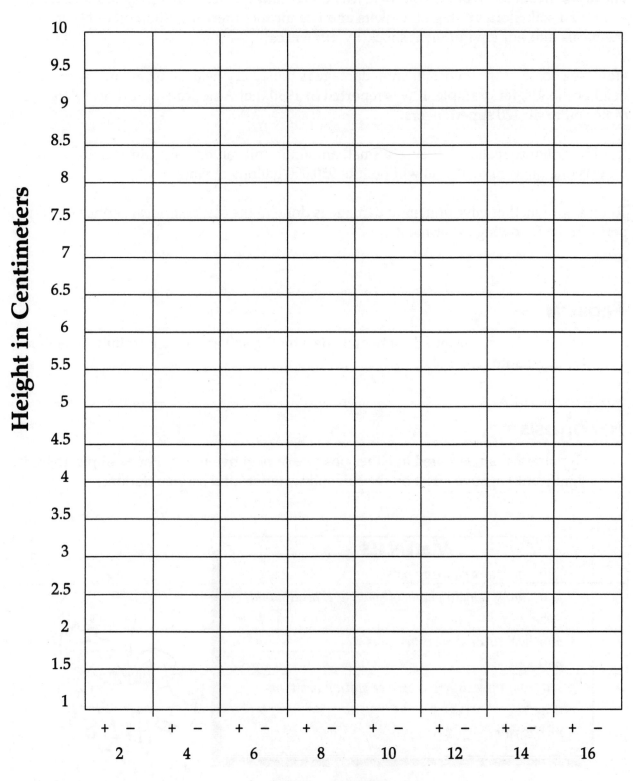

Height in Centimeters

10
9.5
9
8.5
8
7.5
7
6.5
6
5.5
5
4.5
4
3.5
3
2.5
2
1.5
1

+ − + − + − + − + − + − + − + −
2   4   6   8   10   12   14   16

Time in Hours

GASOLINE ALLEY

The news media has reported on toxic waste sites and the harm that they can do to our water and soil. Stories of big oil tankers and chemical refineries spilling oil or other chemicals into our environment shock TV audiences.

However, some of the environmental damage is done very near to us, in our towns or neighborhoods, for example. It was reported in 1990 that Americans threw away enough motor oil to fill 120 supertankers.

It is important to realize that even a small amount of oil can damage our resources. As little as one quart of motor oil will pollute 950,000 gallons of water.

To find out whether environmental damage is done to the soil near local service stations, perform the following experiment.

PROBLEM

Is there a detectable and detrimental effect on the soil and water around a gasoline station or auto repair shop?

HYPOTHESIS

Hypotheses can be stated in either positive or negative terms. For example, there is a significant negative effect on the soil and water around service stations.

MATERIALS
- *four one-quart planting pots*
- *four young tomato plants of equal age, health, and size*
- *four buckets or large coffee cans*
- *potting soil*
- *soil from three different service station locations*
- *water*
- *metric ruler*

PROCEDURE

1. Obtain soil from near three local service stations. Each collection should provide enough soil to fill a one-quart pot for a tomato plant as well as one third of a large coffee can or bucket to be used for watering. The sites should be gasoline stations or auto repair shops. The sites could also be junkyards where motor oil or gasoline has leaked under cars or machinery. The soil selected for each sample should be from as close to the work area as possible. For example, use the area where the water runs off most heavily after the station or shop has been cleaned.

2. Fill each of the four pots with the different soil samples collected. Three samples will be from the service stations and one will be filled with regular potting soil. Be certain to mark each pot with the name of the location of the soil sample.

3. Plant each of the four tomato plants in the four prepared quart-sized pots, according to directions.

4. At the beginning of the experiment use a metric ruler to measure the height in centimeters of each of the four plants and record the heights on the chart provided.

5. In procedure #1, soil samples were collected to fill one third of a bucket or coffee can with water. Fill the remaining two thirds of each bucket or coffee can with water. This is done to imitate the ground water a plant at a given site would have available. Be certain the cans are marked as to the collection site of the soil sample. Do not forget to fill one bucket or coffee can with a one-third to two-thirds combination of regular potting soil and water, respectively.

6. Using the water in the bucket or coffee cans, water each plant with one-half cup of water every three days, beginning with the first day. Replace the water that is used from the buckets or coffee cans.

The tomato plants in potting soil should receive water from the can that contains potting soil and water. The other three tomato plants should receive water from their respective soil and water combinations.

7. Using a metric ruler, measure the height of each tomato plant in centimeters every three days and record the height on the chart provided.

8. Continue the experiment for three weeks.

RESULTS

Plot a line of the growth record of each plant in the experiment on the line graph provided. There will be a total of four lines on the graph, one for each plant in the experiment.

Use different colors on the graph to represent different plants in the experiment.

CONCLUSION

By studying the graph, determine the overall health and growth of the tomato plants grown in different conditions of soil and water.

Articulate the health and growth differences among the plants.

SOIL SURVEY

Record the height of each plant in centimeters

Location	Day 0	Day 3	Day 6	Day 9	Day 12	Day 15	Day 18	Day 21
Site 1 _____								
Site 2 _____								
Site 3 _____								
Potting Soil								

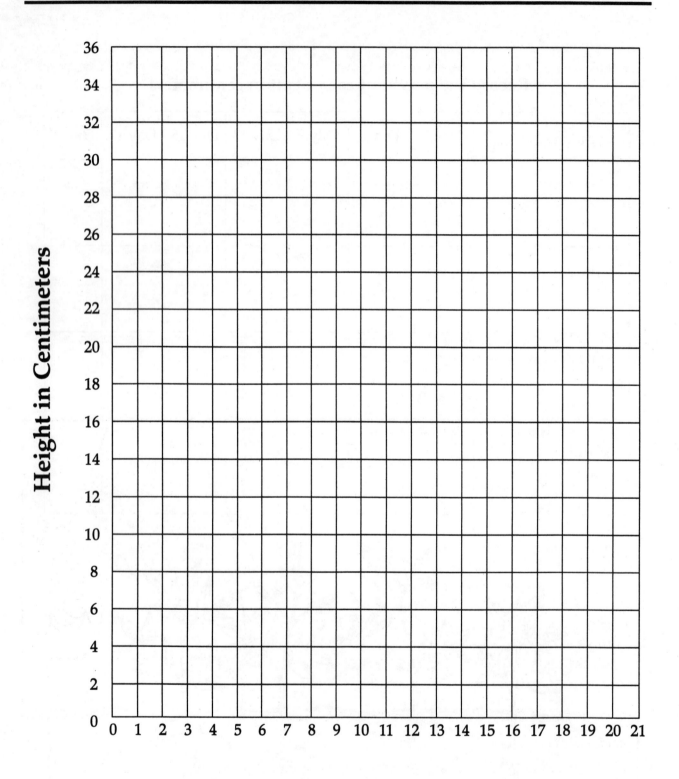

Days

BATTERY BATTLE

Americans buy 2 billion batteries every year. This means that every person in the country uses about eight batteries a year. In a family of four, that calculates to 32 batteries a year.

When we go to the store to buy batteries, there are many types from which to choose. Alkaline, regular, and rechargeable batteries are all choices. There are also options among different brands and price ranges.

The experiment below is a way to test the different batteries to determine which ones work the best and which ones work the longest.

PROBLEM

Which battery works the longest?

HYPOTHESIS

State the type of battery that you believe will last the longest. For example, in a comparison test, alkaline batteries will last the longest.

MATERIALS

- six sets of batteries (Choose the size that is right for your toy or flashlight. Most flashlights and toys require two batteries. Be certain to check your toy or flashlight to find out how many batteries are needed for it to operate. This will be considered a set. Various batteries can be purchased at grocery stores or discount department stores.)
  - a. two sets of heavy-duty batteries
  - b. two sets of alkaline batteries
  - c. two sets of lithium batteries
- battery-operated toy or flashlight (The toy should be a constant-action toy, such as a stuffed dog that wags its tail or barks without stopping until it is turned off.)

PROCEDURE

1. Purchase six sets of batteries for the constant action toy or flashlight. This experiment requires two sets of the three types of batteries. Be certain to check for similar expiration dates on all the different types of batteries. This is very important to ensure the best performance from the battery.

2. Following the manufacturer's directions, place the first set of batteries in the toy or flashlight. Check the time and record it on the chart provided. Immediately turn on the toy or flashlight.

3. Try to begin the experiment when the toy or flashlight can operate continuously for several hours.

4. If you have to leave your toy or flashlight, or go to sleep, and will not be able to detect when the battery runs out, turn off the toy or flashlight. Record the time on the chart provided. Begin the experiment again at an appropriate time. When you start again, remember to check the time, record it, and then immediately turn on the toy or flashlight.

5. While the toy or flashlight is running, check it at least every 15 minutes to make certain the batteries are still operative. When the toy has completely stopped, or the flashlight is completely off, record the time on the chart.

6. To ensure accuracy, replace the set of batteries with the exact same type and repeat the experiment. Again, record the results on the chart.

7. Next, place a set of the second type of batteries in the toy or flashlight. Record the beginning and ending times on the chart as the toy or flashlight is used. Do this for both sets of the second type of batteries.

8. Finally, place a set of the third type of batteries in the toy or flashlight. Again, record the beginning and ending times on the chart as the toy or flashlight is used. Do this for both sets of the third type of batteries.

RESULTS

Use the chart and calculate the average time (in minutes) required for the different types of batteries to use all of their energy.

Using the sheet provided, construct a bar graph of the average number of minutes each type of battery is able to operate.

Using different colors to represent each of the batteries will help clarify the results on the bar graph.

CONCLUSION

By studying the completed bar graph, determine the type of battery that has the longest life. Was the hypothesis of the experiment proved correct or incorrect?

It might also be interesting to report on the cost of the batteries as it relates to their life expectancy.

CHARGE CHART

Battery Type	Time On	Time Off	Time On	Time Off	Time On	Time Off	Total Time	Average Time
Heavy Duty #1								
Heavy Duty #2								
Alkaline #1								
Alkaline #2								
Lithium #1								
Lithium #2								

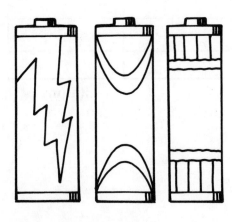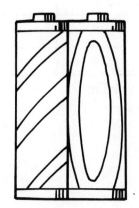

BATTERY BATTLE

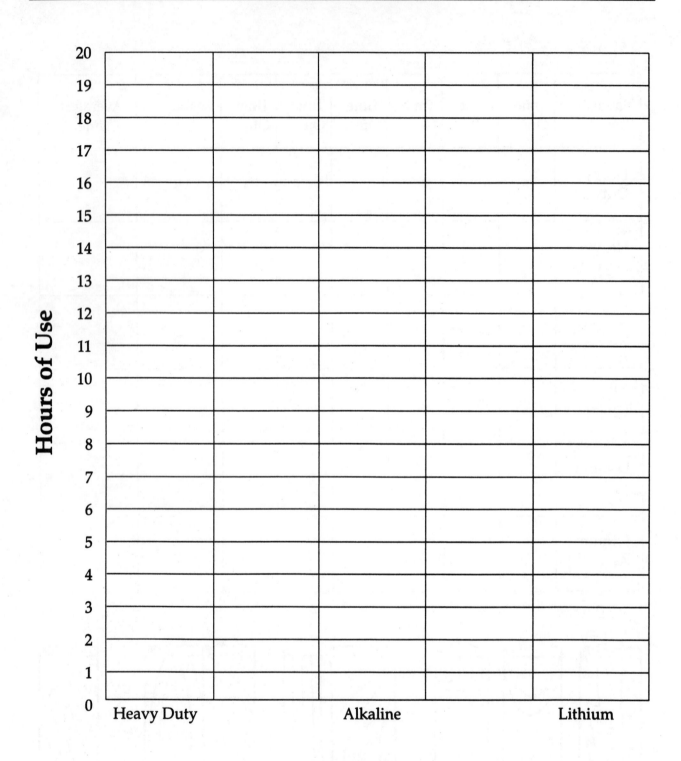

Battery Type

MISSION IMPOPPIBLE

There are many different brands of popcorn on the market. Some are called "gourmet" and are more expensive than others. Some brands are old and reliable. What all brands have in common is that after the popcorn is popped, a few duds are left. Duds are the unpopped kernels of popcorn. Consumers want to purchase reasonably priced popcorn that tastes light and fluffy with a minimal number of duds. There are many brands from which to choose, so how is the best one selected?

The experiment below can help you select the best popcorn.

PROBLEM

Which brand of popping corn is the best? Which brand leaves behind the fewest duds?

HYPOTHESIS

Select the brand of popcorn that will taste the best and leave the fewest duds. For example, Orville Redenbacher will be the best popcorn with the smallest number of unpopped kernels.

MATERIALS

- Orville Redenbacher's Gourmet Popping Corn
- a generic brand of popping corn
- two other brands of popping corn (avoid microwave popcorn)
- popcorn popper
- canola oil
- measuring cup
- measuring spoons
- straight cylinder pitcher
- four popcorn bowls
- appropriate seasoning (optional)
- glue

PROCEDURE

1. Purchase popcorn for the experiment. Include Orville Redenbacher's Gourmet Popping Corn, a generic brand of popping corn, and two other typical brands of popping corn. Avoid microwave popping corn because it is prepackaged.

2. Measure ½ cup of popcorn and the appropriate amount of canola oil according to the directions. Try to use the same amount of popcorn and oil for each brand of popcorn.

3. Follow the cooking instructions for preparing the popcorn.

4. After the popcorn has popped, place each brand of popcorn in a separate bowl. Label the bowls clearly with the appropriate brand of popcorn.

5. Count the number of unpopped kernels and record the number on the chart provided for each brand. Save the unpopped kernels for each brand to glue onto the bar graph for the presentation of the project.

6. To compare fluffiness from brand to brand, pour each brand of popped corn into a straight cylinder pitcher and record the height in centimeters on the chart provided. Use the same pitcher for all four measurements.

7. Season the popcorn as you usually would. Be certain to season each bowl exactly the same way.

8. Next, rate the taste of the popcorn on the chart provided. Use the following rating scale:
   A = outstanding
   B = good
   C = fair
   D = poor

RESULTS

Using the information about the unpopped kernels on the chart, create a bar graph on the sheet provided that shows the number of duds for each brand. Use four different colors to represent the four different brands of popcorn. This will make the graph easier to read. Next, glue the unpopped kernels from each brand onto the appropriate bar on the bar graph. Evenly distribute them on each of the bars.

CONCLUSION

Read the bar graph and chart to determine the best popcorn. Compare the taste and fluffiness of each brand of popcorn. Also, consider the cost of each brand as you are rating the best popcorn overall.

TOPPING THE POP CHARTS

Brand Name	Unpopped Kernels	Taste	Fluffiness	Cost

Rating Scale for Taste

A = Outstanding
B = Good
C = Fair
D = Poor

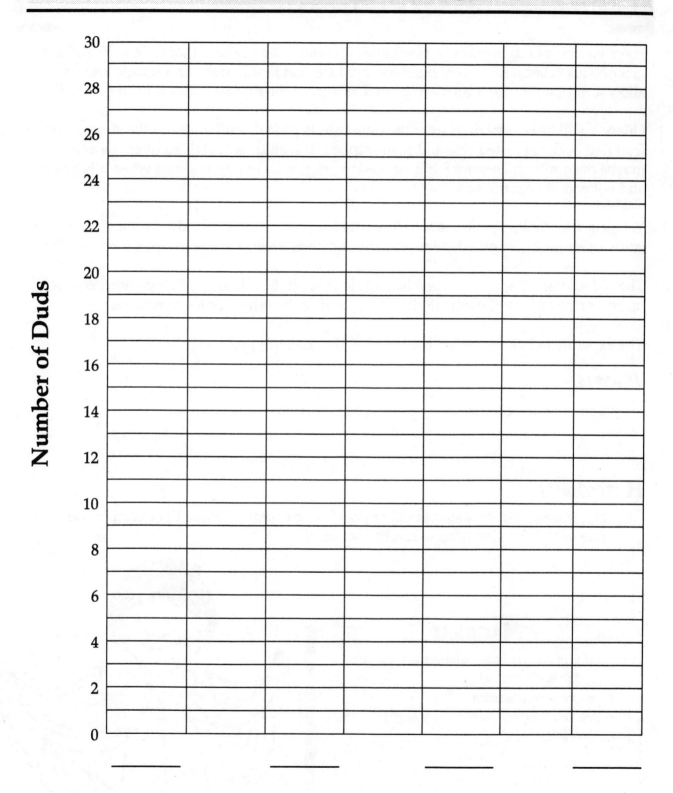

Number of Duds

Brands of Popcorn

RAPID RIPE

Have you ever bought fruits or vegetables in a store and realized that they were still a bit green? This is because grocers purchase produce that is still green and unripe and then allow it to ripen during transport, as well as during the first few days it is on the shelf.

Often, it will be several days from the time fruit is picked until it gets to the store. If the fruit had been harvested ripe and then shipped, it would have arrived overripe and maybe even rotten. Therefore, it is necessary for grocers to buy the fruit when it is green and not completely ripened.

Yet most fruit looks ripe in the store because the green fruit is mixed with the ripe fruit. As fruits ripen they give off ethylene gas, which causes greener fruits to ripen more quickly.

The old saying, "It only takes one bad apple to spoil the whole barrel," is true, because one overripe apple will emit ethylene gas, causing the other apples to ripen early.

The experiment below can test the speed of the ripening process.

PROBLEM

Can the rate of the ripening process be increased?

HYPOTHESIS

Hypotheses can be stated in either positive or negative terms. For example, yes, the rate of the ripening process can be increased.

MATERIALS

- *three of the greenest bananas you can buy (in the same bunch)*
- *one very ripe banana*
- *two small brown bags (lunch bags)*
- *two clothespins*

PROCEDURE

1. Buy one very ripe banana and let it ripen more at home for a couple of days.

2. After the two days have passed, go back to the store to buy three of the greenest bananas you can find in the same bunch.

3. Place one green banana in a brown paper lunch bag with the very ripe banana. Fold at the top and close with a clothespin. Mark the bag "A."

4. Place one green banana in a brown paper lunch bag by itself. Fold at the top and close with a clothespin. Place this bag at least one foot away from the first bag. Mark the bag "B."

5. Place the last green banana on the counter by itself, at least one foot away from the other two bags. Place a card marked "C" beside the banana.

6. Look at the peel of each of the green bananas every morning (M) and every evening (E). Record the ripening process of each banana on the chart provided. Use the following rating scale:
   G = green
   Y = yellow
   S = spotted
   B = brown, to indicate the maximum ripeness

7. Continue the experiment until the peels of all three green bananas reach the color brown, indicating maximum ripeness.

RESULTS

Be certain to complete the chart, recording all the information about the banana peel's color, beginning with green and ending with brown. Make a bar graph on the sheet provided, graphing the number of days it took for each green banana to reach the maximum ripeness of brown.

CONCLUSION

View the chart and consider whether or not the pace of the ripening can be increased. Was your hypothesis correct?

Can you think of applications for this experiment with other fruits and vegetables you purchase?

GOING BANANAS

Banana	Day 1 M E	Day 2 M E	Day 3 M E	Day 4 M E	Day 5 M E	Day 6 M E	Day 7 M E	Day 8 M E	Day 9 M E	Day 10 M E	Day 11 M E	Day 12 M E	Day 13 M E	Day 14 M E
Banana A														
Banana B														
Banana C														

Rating Scale for the Banana Peel:

G = Green
Y = Yellow
S = Spotted
B = Brown

A PEELING GRAPH

Number of Days

Group A   Group B   Group C

Banana Groups

ANT BAIT

Ants can be fun to watch and learn from, in ant farms or just in your own backyard. Ants can also be a nuisance at picnics and other outdoor activities. Ants often make nests in inconvenient places.

Since ants can be a nuisance, sometimes we want to get rid of them. To accomplish this, chemicals are often used. If the entire nest is to be killed, the ants have to carry a poison deep into the nest to reach the queen. They will do this only if they think the poison is food or if the poison is mixed into a food.

But which food attracts the most ants? Once we know, then ant poison can be mixed into ant food, creating a bait. Obviously, pesticide companies are quite interested in this information.

The experiment below is designed to discover which type of food ants prefer in order to create the best bait.

PROBLEM

What food attracts the most ants?

HYPOTHESIS

Choose a pure food like sugar, fat, a food high in protein (lunch meat), or a carbohydrate. If you choose a donut, which has fat, sugar, and carbohydrate, you would not get a clear answer. Therefore, a pure food is more effective. The hypothesis might be, for example, sugar will attract the most ants.

MATERIALS
- *pasta (carbohydrate)*
- *rice (carbohydrate)*
- *bacon fat*
- *chicken skin (fat)*
- *sugar*
- *honey*
- *lean lunch meat (protein)*
- *sugar-free Knox gelatin (protein)*
- *eight flat, plastic lids (from butter tubs or coffee cans)*

PROCEDURE

1. Cook the pasta and rice separately. Set aside.

2. Remove the fat from two slices of bacon and set aside.

3. Remove the skin of a chicken and set aside.

4. Prepare Knox gelatin (sugar-free) according to package directions. Allow it to harden.

5. Wait for a warm, sunny day when the ants are more likely to be out. Ants will come out on cloudy days, but do not conduct the experiment on a rainy day.

6. Place the food on the eight flat, plastic lids, one food per lid.

7. Find an area in your yard (or in the yard of your school or church) that will not be disturbed by people or pets during the course of the experiment.

8. Set the flat plastic lids of food in the pattern shown below. The pattern is arranged so that the similar food types are not next to one another. This way the ants will not be attracted to the closest food, but to their actual food preference. Place each food item eight inches from any other food.

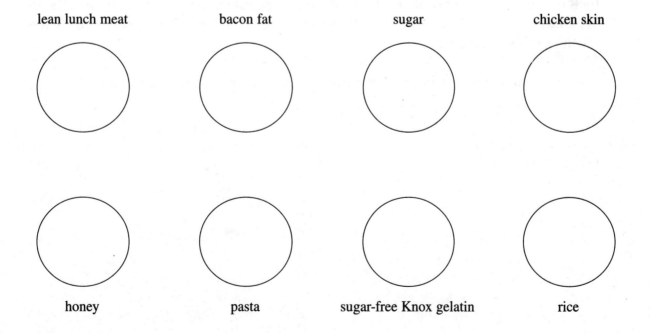

lean lunch meat   bacon fat   sugar   chicken skin

honey   pasta   sugar-free Knox gelatin   rice

9. Record the time you begin the experiment on the chart provided. You should conduct the experiment on the morning of a day you plan to be home for at least 12 consecutive hours.

10. Every hour, count the number of ants on the flat, plastic lids. Record the number of ants on the chart provided. If the ants have formed a trail, count only the ants on the flat plastic lid. If there are too many ants to count quickly, place the flat plastic lid in the freezer for two minutes. The ants will be cold and slow, making it easier to count them. After counting the ants, return the flat, plastic lid to its spot in the experiment.

11. Continue the experiment for 12 hours.

RESULTS

Using the chart, create a line graph of the average number of ants found each hour on the two fats, the two sugars, the two carbohydrates, and the two proteins. Be certain to use different colors for each line on the line graph so that it will be more clear.

CONCLUSION

By looking at the line graph, draw a conclusion about the food to which the ants are most attracted. Consider your hypothesis once again. What can be explained by the results of this experiment?

Also, consider how this information might apply to ant poisons and ant baits.

GETTING ANTSY

Record the number of ants on each food every hour

Food	Hr. 1	Hr. 2	Hr. 3	Hr. 4	Hr. 5	Hr. 6	Hr. 7	Hr. 8	Hr. 9	Hr. 10	Hr. 11	Hr. 12
Pasta (starch)												
Rice (starch)												
Average												
Sugar Cube												
Honey (sugar)												
Average												
Bacon (fat)												
Chicken Skin (fat)												
Average												
Lunch Meat (protein)												
Gelatin (protein)												
Average												

FOODS ANTS CHOOSE

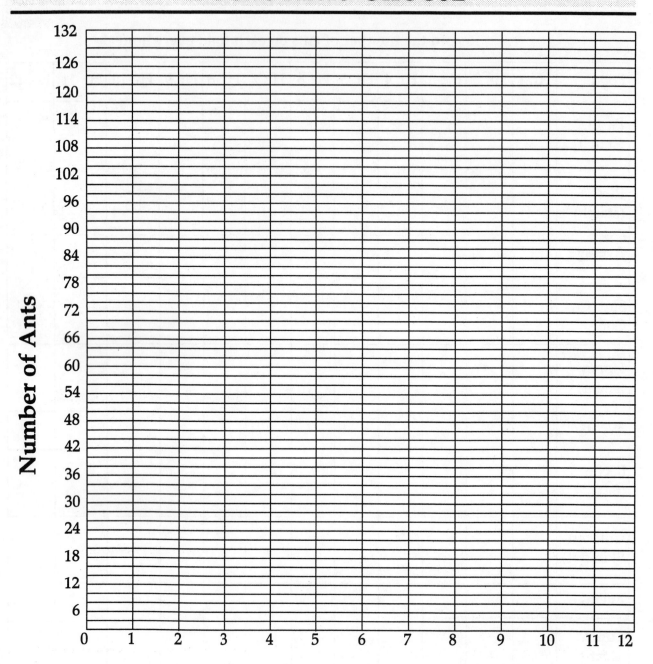

Number of Ants

132 126 120 114 108 102 96 90 84 78 72 66 60 54 48 42 36 30 24 18 12 6

0 1 2 3 4 5 6 7 8 9 10 11 12

Hours

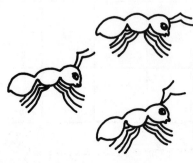

Starch = _____ Colored Line

Protein = _____ Colored Line

Fats = _____ Colored Line

Sugar = _____ Colored Line

IT'S TV TIME

Most homes in America have a television set. Many homes have more than one. Even some vehicles come equipped with a television and VCR.

In schools, televisions and VCRs are used to present films and other educational shows. There are appropriate television shows and videotapes for every subject in school.

Without a doubt, the television is a typical part of American life. Sometimes parents and others become concerned that people watch too much television. Many professionals agree that we should limit television viewing. They also agree that we should carefully plan our television program schedule.

The problem in this experiment is determining how much television and how many videos your family watches in a typical week. This experiment helps you to discover how much time your family spends watching television in a week. Of course, you will need the cooperation of your family!

PROBLEM

How much TV does your family watch in a typical day and week? On which day does the television get the heaviest usage?

HYPOTHESIS

Consider your family's habits and write down the number of hours a week you think your family watches television. Also, consider which day of the week the television has the heaviest usage. For example, my family watches 30 hours of television a week, viewing the most on Monday.

MATERIALS

- *all the televisions in your home*
- *a 24-hour appliance timer for every television in the experiment (These can be purchased at a discount department store.)*
- *the outlet used for each of the televisions in the experiment*

PROCEDURE

1. Set the 24-hour appliance timer at 12:00.

2. Plug the television into the 24-hour appliance timer. If there is more than one television in the experiment, each one should have its own timer. Each timer should be set at 12:00.

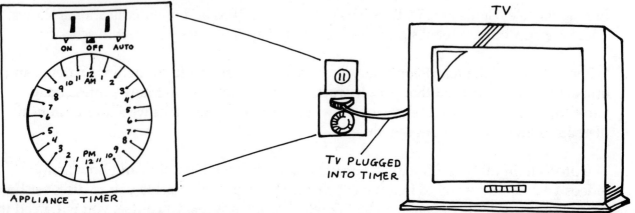

3. For the duration of the experiment, the televisions will be turned on and off by plugging the 24-hour timer into the wall outlets that the televisions are usually plugged into.

4. If the television(s) has a remote control, tape a piece of paper to the power button on the remote control so that whoever watches the television will remember to turn it on and off with the timer at the outlet. In addition, tape a note to the power button on the front of each of the TVs.

5. Every day at the same time, check the 24-hour appliance timers by counting the number of hours that passed from the original 12:00 settings. If there is more

than one television in the home, add the times of all the appliance timers. This is the number of hours that the televisions and VCRs have been on in the last 24 hours. Record this amount of time to the closest minute on the chart provided. Reset the timers to the 12:00 setting.

6. It is imperative, for this experiment to be successful, that the televisions are always turned on and off at the wall outlet and that the appliance timer is reset to 12:00 after its daily check at the same time.

7. Run the experiment for two weeks so that an average can be calculated.

RESULTS

Calculate the average amount of time the household watched videos and television for each day of the week. Record this number on the chart in the space marked "Average Viewing Times." Then calculate the weekly average of time that your family watches television by adding together all the daily averages. Record the numbers on the appropriate spaces on the chart.

Next, create a bar graph on the sheet provided showing the average number of hours spent watching television per day. Be certain to use a different color for each day of the week to make the graph more clear.

CONCLUSION

View the chart and the bar graph. Determine whether the hypothesis about the number of hours per week spent by your family watching television was accurate.

Also, note whether the experiment's prediction about the day of heaviest television usage was correct. This can be determined by looking at the tallest bar on the graph.

Do the results from this experiment surprise you or members of your family? If your family is watching more television than predicted, do you foresee any changes in the future, such as planning a program schedule?

MASHING COUCH POTATOES

Days of the Week	Week One Viewing Times	Week Two Viewing Times	Average Viewing Times
Sunday			
Monday			
Tuesday			
Wednesday			
Thursday			
Friday			
Saturday			
Weekly Totals			

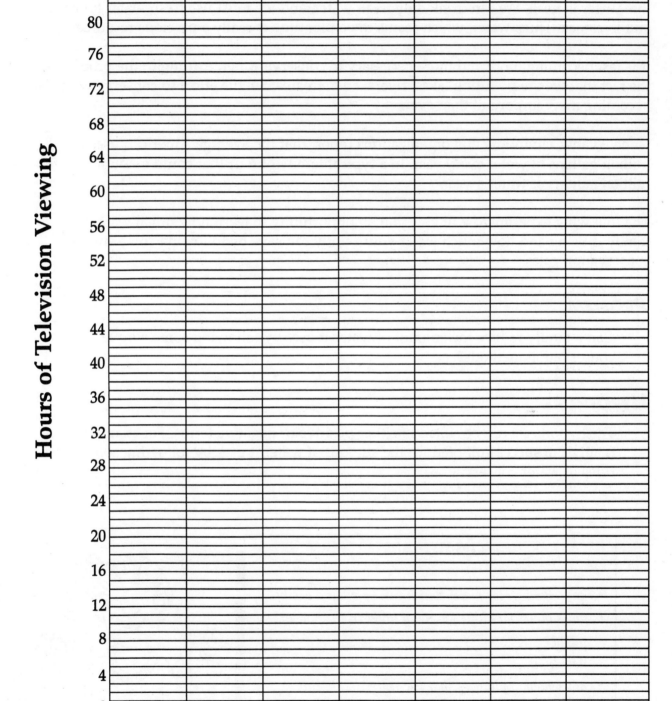

Days of the Week

DOWN THE DRAIN

Three quarters of the earth's surface is covered with water; however, only one percent of that water is fresh. We can drink only fresh water, and we must use fresh water for crops and livestock. Thus, water, which seems to be plentiful, is really a precious resource.

It is fast becoming more and more necessary to conserve water. Adding to the problem is the fact that we are polluting lakes, rivers, and streams. So, the effort to conserve water is becoming more important than ever.

Unbelievably, environmental organizations report that the average American uses two million gallons of water every year. In a typical family of four that could amount to eight million gallons of water a year.

The following experiment will give you an opportunity to learn how much water your family is using and how much water your family can save by following some simple conservation rules.

PROBLEM

Can a family reduce the amount of water it uses by following some simple conservation methods?

HYPOTHESIS

The hypothesis can be stated in either positive or negative terms. For example, a family can successfully reduce the amount of water it uses by following some simple rules of water conservation.

MATERIALS

- *household water meter which can be viewed easily*
- *glass quart jars (one for every toilet in the house)*
- *pitcher*
- *flashlight*
- *household appliances that use water (sink, tub, dishwasher, washer for laundry, and garden hose)*

PROCEDURE

Part I. Monitoring Water Usage

1. Find the water meter at your home. It may be in one of three locations. It may be located in the corner of the basement, on the outside wall of your house, or in the yard near the street or road under a cement or metal cover.

   If it is under a cover, remove the cover and read the water meter dial and record the number of gallons on the chart. The meter is read in gallons. There is also a way to read $\frac{1}{10}$ of a gallon on the outer side of the meter.

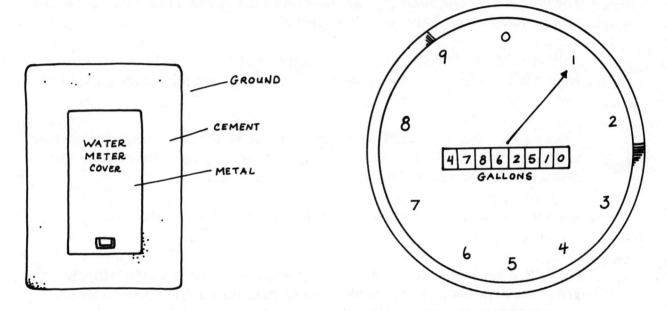

2. Go to the water meter at the same time every day and record the number of gallons used since the previous day on the chart provided. Do this for one week.

3. At the end of that week, calculate the total number of gallons of water used by the household during the week and record this figure on the chart provided. It is important that the family is not aware that its water usage is being monitored during this week. Once the amount of water being used is calculated for the week, go to Part II.

Part II. The Conservation Effort

1. Begin with the toilets in the house. Toilets account for about 40 percent of household water use. An average flush requires about five to seven gallons of water. That amount can be reduced by placing an open quart jar in the tank of every toilet in the house.

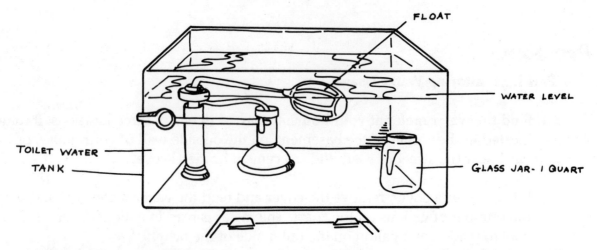

FLOAT

WATER LEVEL

TOILET WATER
TANK

GLASS JAR- 1 QUART

The jar will save one quart of water for every flush in the household. So a gallon of water can be saved after only four flushes.

2. Enlist your family's help to shorten the amount of time spent in the shower, as well as taking a shower rather than a bath. This will also reduce the amount of water used.

3. Once again, enlist the help of your family to save water by turning off the water while brushing teeth rather than allowing it to run. Use the running water for rinsing the toothbrush and mouth only.

The same technique can be used for individuals who have to shave every morning.

4. Next, fill a pitcher or bottle with drinking water and place it in the refrigerator. When someone wants a cool drink of water, pour it from the pitcher instead of running the tap water and waiting for it to get cool.

5. When washing dishes in the sink, do not leave the water running. Simply place enough water in the sink to cover the dishes.

When using the dishwasher, wait until it is full before running it.

6. Look for leaks around the house. Check toilets and faucets. Also, check underneath the sinks for leaks.

Leaks can be costly. A leak that can fill up a coffee cup in ten minutes will waste over 3,000 gallons of water in a year.

Another way to check for leaks is to write down the number of gallons shown on the water meter right before everyone leaves the house. When everyone returns, check the water meter again. If the number has changed, then there may very well be a leak somewhere.

7. When it is time to water the lawn, garden, or other plants, be certain to water in the early morning or late evening to reduce the amount of evaporation. Less water waste will occur and more water will be used by the plants. Try not to water on a windy day since the wind will speed up the evaporation process. Also, if a sprinkler is used, try to place it in such a way to reduce the amount of runoff that occurs.

8. When washing laundry, be certain that the setting for the size of the load is correct. This way the washing machine will not waste water by filling all the way up for a small load.

9. Once your family has agreed to the conservation effort and leaks are repaired, begin a new week of monitoring water usage. The amount of water used during a regular week will be compared with the amount of water used by the household while following simple conservation rules. Go to the water meter and record the number of gallons on the chart provided to begin monitoring the conservation week.

10. Check the water meter every day at the same time. Record the number of gallons used since the previous day on the chart. Do this in the same way that you monitored the water usage during the regular week.

RESULTS

View the completed chart for the normal week of water usage versus the water conservation week. Calculate how much water the family saved on each day of the week by following simple conservation rules. Next, add together all the gallons of water saved each day to determine how much water the family saved in a week.

Finally, multiply the weekly number of gallons your family saved by water conservation by 52 (52 weeks in a year) to calculate how many gallons of water your family could save in a year.

CONCLUSION

Create a bar graph with two bars for each day of the week. One bar for each day of the week will be red to show how many gallons of water were used by your family on a normal day. The other bar will be blue to reveal how many gallons of water were used a day by your family during the water conservation effort. This graph will clarify a comparison of regular water usage versus water usage following some simple conservation rules.

Finally, hold a family meeting to show the results of your experiment. Discuss with your family the differences the household experienced in water usage by following some easy conservation rules. You may want to remind your family that conserving water is not only good for the environment, but it saves money as well! (Suggest a family outing with the money saved.)

WATER WATCHER

Week	Initial Meter Reading	Gallons Used During Day 1	Gallons Used During Day 2	Gallons Used During Day 3	Gallons Used During Day 4	Gallons Used During Day 5	Gallons Used During Day 6	Gallons Used During Day 7	Total Gallons Used in the Week	Total Gallons Used in a Year
Regular Week										
Conservation Week										
Water Saved										

DON'T BE A DRIP

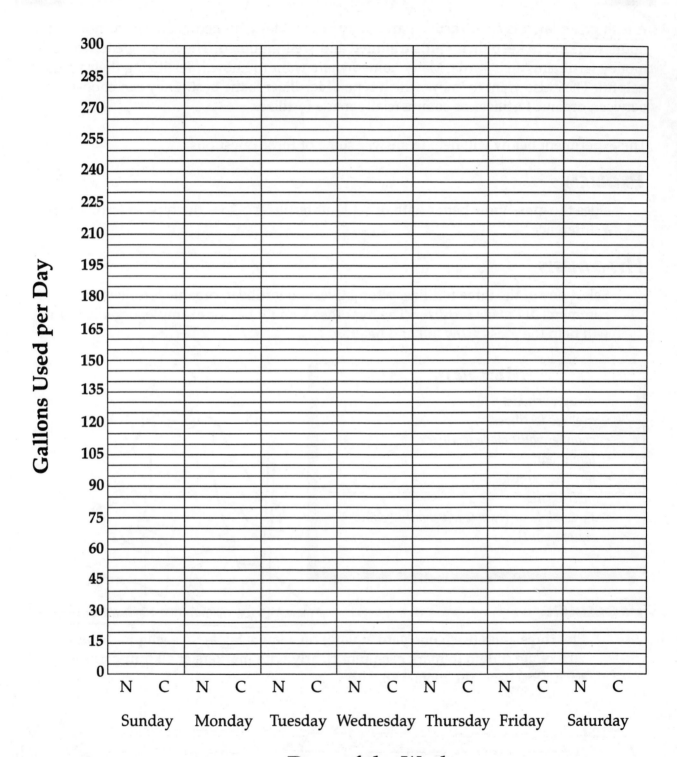

Gallons Used per Day

300
285
270
255
240
225
210
195
180
165
150
135
120
105
90
75
60
45
30
15
0

N   C   N   C   N   C   N   C   N   C   N   C   N   C

Sunday   Monday   Tuesday   Wednesday   Thursday   Friday   Saturday

Days of the Week

N = Graph of Normal Water Usage   C = Graph of Water Usage While Conserving

WATCHING THE GRASS GROW

A lush green lawn is an attractive part of any home. Many homeowners spend hours and hours working to keep their yards trimmed and well-groomed. They also spend time and money fertilizing their yards. Many homeowners want to know if fertilizing their yards is helpful. They also want to know which type of fertilizer is the best. They can choose between organic fertilizer or commercially made fertilizer.

The experiment below will help to answer some of these questions.

PROBLEM

Does the grass grow better with or without fertilizer? Does the type of fertilizer make a difference?

HYPOTHESIS

Select one of the three fertilizer alternatives: no fertilizer, organic fertilizer, or commercially made fertilizer. The hypothesis might be, for example, organic fertilizer will help the grass grow tall and healthy.

MATERIALS

- water sprinkler
- organic fertilizer
- commercially made fertilizer
- lawn markers
- fertilizer spreader
- metric ruler
- three plots of grass (each should be one square yard)

PROCEDURE

1. Plot three areas (each one yard square) on a lawn. Separate each plot by at least 20 feet. Be certain to mark each plot clearly with markers at all four corners of each plot. Label the plots A, B, and C.

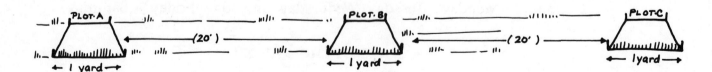

2. With the supervision of an adult, mow all three plots of grass.

3. Using a metric ruler, measure the height of the grass in millimeters by setting the ruler on the dirt and reading the height. Do this for each of three plots and record the height on the chart provided.

4. Do not fertilize plot A.

5. Fertilize plot B with organic fertilizer. Use the fertilizer spreader to spread the amount recommended.

6. Fertilize plot C with commercially made fertilizer. Use the fertilizer spreader to spread the amount recommended. Remember that the plots should be far enough away from one another that water runoff from one will not affect another.

7. Every two days water each plot with a water sprinkler for about 20 minutes. It is best to water early in the morning or late in the evening. Be certain to sprinkle water on each plot for an equal amount of time.

8. Every two days measure the height of the grass in each plot and record on the chart provided. Use the metric ruler to measure in millimeters.

9. Continue the experiment for two weeks. Do not mow plots A, B, or C during this time.

*Note: This experiment works best in the spring or early fall.

RESULTS

Using the chart, create a line graph for each of the three plots of grass. Use a different color for each line to highlight each of the three plots of grass. For example, use green for the plot that did not receive fertilizer, use blue for the plot that received organic fertilizer, and use red for the plot that received commercially made fertilizer.

CONCLUSION

View the line graph. Look to see if there are discernable differences in the height and health of the three plots of grass. Did the fertilizer really make a difference? Did the organic fertilizer work more effectively than the commercially made fertilizer? What will you recommend to someone working on attaining a lush and attractive lawn?

FERTILIZER FUN

Record the growth of grass in millimeters.

Grass Plot	Day 0	Day 2	Day 4	Day 6	Day 8	Day 10	Day 12	Day 14
No Fertilizer A								
Organic Fertilizer B								
Commercial Fertilizer C								

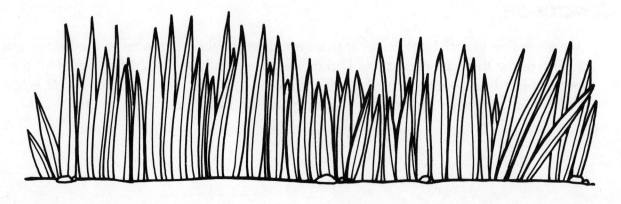

PLOTTING PLOTS

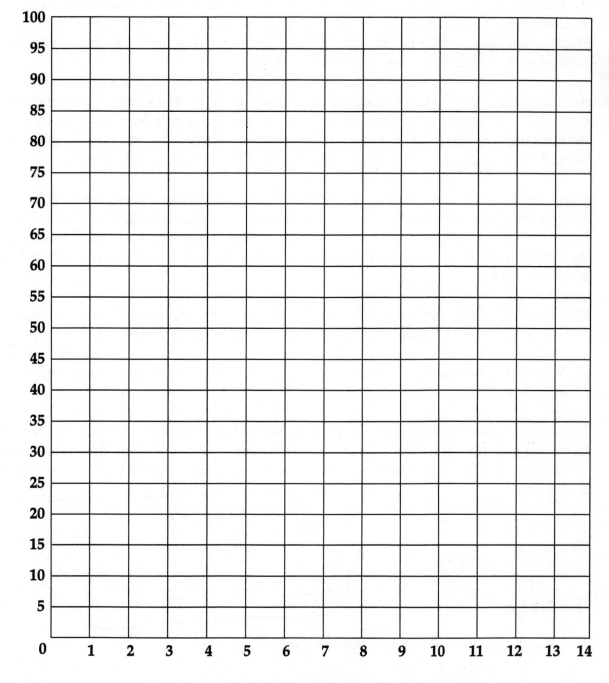

Days of Experiment

A = Plot that received no fertilizer _____ colored line

B = Plot that received organic fertilizer _____ colored line

C = Plot that received commercial fertilizer _____ colored line

THE FUNGUS AMONG US

We have all had the experience of reaching into the refrigerator for a snack, only to discover the food we wanted to eat looked fuzzy. Or maybe we have pulled a slice of bread out of the bag only to find blue or black spots growing on it. The fuzzy growth or colored spots on old food is mold, a type of fungi.

Another unsightly problem is mildew, which may grow in the tub and between tiles in the bathroom, a moist and warm environment. All fungi prefer a dark, warm, and moist environment. Molds, mildew, and even the common mushrooms, are all examples of fungi. However, not all fungi are problems. In fact, fungi can be quite helpful.

Fungi serve an important role in the environment. Fungi are decomposers They help convert materials, such as left-over food, fruit and vegetable peelings, egg shells, old leaves, and grass clippings, back into soil so that they can be reused. Even big trees, once they die, begin to rot, decay, and decompose back into the soil. Fungus is one of nature's ways to recycle.

Some families build compost piles as a form of household recycling. When the organic waste, like fruit and vegetable peelings, unused food from the kitchen, grass clippings, and other yard waste, is placed in the compost pile, it decomposes and can be used in gardens and flower beds. It is like using a natural fertilizer to promote the health of plants.

Sometimes, however, fungus begins to form on food items before we want it to. The following experiment will explore some possible methods for slowing down the process of decomposition. The experiment will also look at where food should be stored in order to slow decay.

PROBLEM

Can the growth of mold on food be slowed?

HYPOTHESIS

Select a substance from the list of materials that will be the most effective in slowing the growth of mold.

MATERIALS

- two or three potatoes
- apple corer
- cotton balls
- plastic wrap
- straight pin
- twenty small clean glass jars
- tweezers
- ammonia
- alcohol
- dish soap
- bleach
- orange juice
- apple juice
- whole milk
- article of clothing
- water

PROCEDURE

1. Use the apple corer and make 20 equal-sized cores from the potatoes.

2. Place enough moistened cotton balls to cover the bottom of each small clean glass jar. This is done because fungi prefer moisture to grow.

3. Label two jars in each of the following ways: undisturbed, ammonia, rubbing alcohol, dish soap, bleach, water, orange juice, apple juice, whole milk, and clothing.

4. Using the tweezers, take two potato cores and place one in each of the jars marked "undisturbed." The potato will be set directly on the moistened cotton balls.

5. Using tweezers, take two potato cores and dip them in ammonia. Blot the excess ammonia. Place one potato in each of the jars marked "ammonia."

6. Using tweezers, take two potato cores and dip them in rubbing alcohol. Blot the excess alcohol and place one potato in each of the jars marked "alcohol."

7. Partially fill a sink with warm water and dish soap. Swirl it around to get frothy bubbles. Using tweezers, take two potato cores and dip them in the sink filled with warm water and dish soap bubbles. Blot the excess bubbles. Place one potato in each of the jars marked "dish soap."

MOISTENED
COTTON BALLS

POTATO

8. Using tweezers, take two potato cores and dip them in bleach. Blot the excess bleach, and place one potato in each of the jars marked "bleach."

9. Using tweezers, take two potato cores and dip them in plain warm water. Blot the excess water. Place one potato in each of the jars marked "water."

10. Using tweezers, take two potato cores and dip them in orange juice. Blot the excess orange juice. Place one potato in each of the jars marked "orange juice."

11. Using tweezers, take two potato cores and dip them in apple juice. Blot the excess apple juice. Place one potato in each of the jars marked "apple juice."

12. Using tweezers, take two potato cores and dip them in whole milk. Blot the excess milk, and place one potato in each of the jars marked "whole milk."

13. Place two potato cores on an article of clothing that is placed in the laundry hamper after being worn. Let all sides of the potato touch the clothing. Using tweezers, place one potato in each of the jars marked "clothing."

14. Cover the top openings of each jar with plastic wrap. Put a few small pin holes in the plastic wrap.

15. Place one of each type of jar in a warm dark place, such as under the bathroom sink or kitchen sink.

16. Place one of each type of jar in a light place, such as on a kitchen counter. Avoid direct sunlight.

17. Check the jars every day at the same time and check for the presence or absence of mold. Record this information on the chart provided.

18. Continue the experiment for three weeks.

RESULTS

Complete the chart provided to determine when each jar showed mold growth. Also be careful to note differences between the jars in the warm, dark location versus the jars in the light location.

CONCLUSION

View the completed chart. Compare the different substances to determine which one seemed most effective in inhibiting the growth of mold. Which jar showed mold first? Which jar showed mold last? Was there a difference between the jars in the light and dark areas? Does it seem that any substances were able to speed up the appearance of mold? Does it seem that any substances were able to slow the appearance of mold?

Did the light or dark environment make a difference in the appearance of mold?

Check to see if your hypothesis was correct in predicting the best inhibitor of mold growth.

THE ROTTEN WORLD AROUND US

Potato Type	Day 1	Day 2	Day 3	Day 4	Day 5	Day 6	Day 7	Day 8	Day 9	Day 10	Day 11	Day 12	Day 13	Day 14	Day 15	Day 16	Day 17	Day 18	Day 19	Day 20	Day 21
Water (L)																					
Water (D)																					
Bleach (L)																					
Bleach (D)																					
Ammonia (L)																					
Ammonia (D))																					
Alcohol (L)																					
Alcohol (D)																					
Dish Soap (L)																					
Dish Soap (D)																					
Orange Juice (L)																					
Orange Juice (D)																					
Clothing (L)																					
Clothing (D)																					
Milk (L)																					
Milk (D)																					
Apple Juice (L)																					
Apple Juice (D)																					
Undisturbed (L)																					
Undisturbed (D)																					

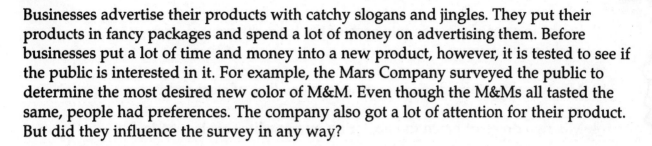

Businesses advertise their products with catchy slogans and jingles. They put their products in fancy packages and spend a lot of money on advertising them. Before businesses put a lot of time and money into a new product, however, it is tested to see if the public is interested in it. For example, the Mars Company surveyed the public to determine the most desired new color of M&M. Even though the M&Ms all tasted the same, people had preferences. The company also got a lot of attention for their product. But did they influence the survey in any way?

The big business of marketing sometimes tries to influence how the public thinks and reacts with its advertising campaigns. Subliminal messages are cues picked up by the subconscious that will influence our decisions.

Can an experiment be run to determine if a seemingly unbiased survey can be influenced or shifted using subliminal signals controlled by the researcher? The experiment below describes how to perform this experiment using various colors of soda pop.

PROBLEM

Can subliminal signals influence a person when making a product choice?

HYPOTHESIS

In this experiment, the color blue will be used in subliminal signals to influence people to prefer blue soda.

MATERIALS

- clear plastic cups
- clear soda (such as 7-Up, Sprite, or Slice)
- blue, red, and green food coloring
- soda crackers (such as saltine crackers)
- light blue paper napkins
- blue and black markers
- light blue poster board (two large sheets)
- blue shirt or other blue apparel (to wear when administering the survey)
- three clear pitchers/containers
- copies of the survey form and pens

PROCEDURE

1. Check with school administration to acquire permission to sponsor a survey of soda pop colors during lunch or before school.

2. Pour the same clear soda into each of the three different clear pitchers/containers.

3. Mix two drops of red food coloring into one liter of clear soda.

4. Mix two drops of green food coloring into one liter of clear soda.

5. Mix five drops (slightly more than the red and green) blue food coloring into two liters of clear soda. This is a subliminal cue.

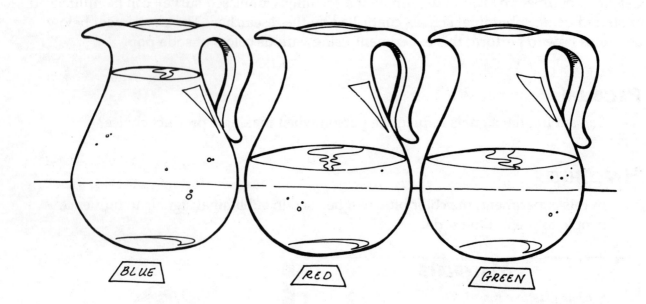

6. Set up a table with small clear plastic cups, about half full of red, green, and blue soda. Pour about ten cups of each color ahead of time to help speed up the distribution process.

7. Make a sign on light blue poster board saying, "Which soda do you like best?" Place it next to your survey table. Also, design a sign using light blue poster board that advertises your survey for selecting colored soda.

8. Wear a blue shirt or other blue apparel on the day of the survey.

9. Place the soda crackers used in the experiment on light blue napkins.

10. Additionally, be certain that the blue soda is either the first or the last in the survey. It should not be in the middle.

11. Give people who wish to participate in the experiment a copy of the enclosed "Soda Survey," which contains instructions for the procedures. It is important that you do not discuss the differences among the drinks with the subjects. Also, ask the subjects in the survey not to discuss the drinks with one another. Simply ask each person to read and follow the instructions. Be certain that the subject takes a bite of soda cracker between each drink of soda.

RESULTS

Collect the completed survey forms and tally the results for each color. Record the number of individuals who chose each color drink on the bottom of the bar graph provided.

On the sheet provided, construct a bar graph of the totals for each color of soda. Color the bars on the bar graph using red, green, and blue to represent the colors of the soda used in the experiment.

CONCLUSION

Study the graph. Were you able to influence the results towards favoring the blue soda by using blue subliminal messages? If not, also consider whether the subjects were negatively influenced by the possible overuse of blue, making it the least chosen soda.

SODA SURVEY

We are testing a new soda today to market some time in the future. We are asking your help to select the most appealing color of this new product.

Please do not discuss this taste test with others, particularly other participants in this survey. Discussing your preferences with other participants may influence people's choices.

Also, please take a bite of soda cracker between each drink of soda to clear the palate.

After tasting all three sodas, select your favorite by placing a check mark next to your choice.

Directions: Place a check mark on the line above your favorite soda color.

_____   _____   _____
   Blue Soda   Red Soda   Green Soda

Thank you for participating in the colored Soda Survey!

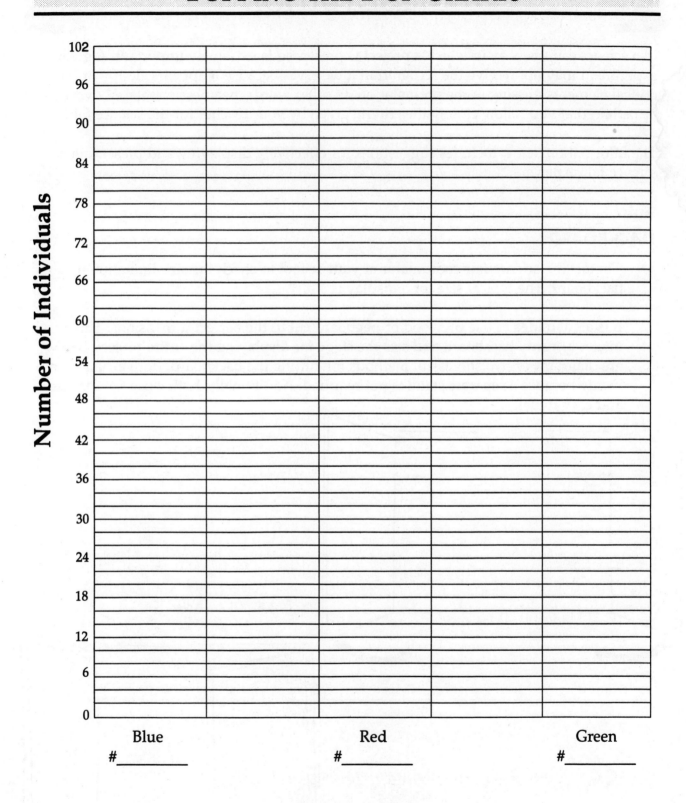

Color of Soda

PRESENTATION

In a science fair, the way in which a project is presented is extremely important. A great experiment may not receive the recognition it deserves because it appears sloppy or has critical elements missing in the presentation. In other words, neatness counts! Above all, be certain that you follow closely the criteria given by your teacher for the science fair.

The information below includes suggestions for effectively displaying and presenting a science fair experiment.

BACKBOARD

Contact the science fair coordinator at your school to check the size limitation for the backboard. The typical size for a display is 3' x 3'.

It is a good idea to use plywood or pegboard cut to the correct dimensions. This makes a sturdy backboard and sets the stage for displaying the entire project. Below are diagrams of two successful methods for cutting the backboard. Both examples are handy because a separate stand is not required. Additionally, both close flat for safe and easy travel.

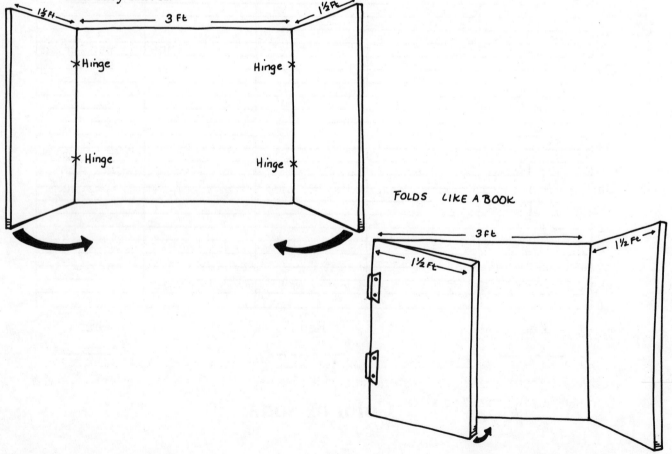

Once the backboard is cut, it should be painted or covered in a solid color. You can paint the backboard a solid color of your choice. Using spray paint is very handy for this.

Another attractive method for decorating the backboard is covering it with a solid colored fabric, such as cotton cloth, burlap, or felt. In order to cover the boards, purchase fabric that extends past each edge of the pegboard or plywood by at least four inches. Lay the board in the middle of the fabric. Begin tacking down the corners securely with glue, thumb tacks, or staples. Once the corners are fastened, fold down each side of the fabric neatly and tightly as if you were wrapping a present.

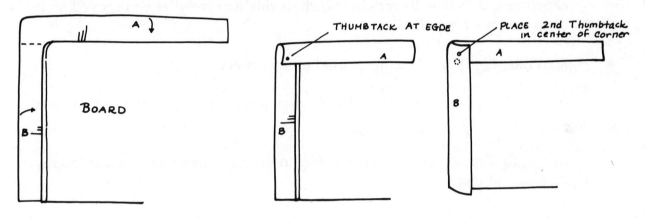

Finally, attach the hinges onto the backboard so that it will conveniently fold for easy transport.

TITLE

The title should be displayed prominently toward the top of the backboard. Large letters help the judges quickly focus on your project. The lettering should be done carefully, not freehand. It is desirable and acceptable to buy stencils or to purchase professionally designed lettering.

Do not forget to place your name beneath the title on the display board so that the project can be identified easily by the judges. Check the rules at your science fair first, since the judges may not want to know who did which project.

SCIENTIFIC METHOD

The six steps of scientific method should be included as elements in the science fair project. Each of the six steps of the scientific method should be enlarged to guide the judges through the experiment.

The letters for each step of the scientific method do not need to be as big as the lettering used for the title, but they should be large enough to be noticed quickly after the title.

The information involved in each step should be placed underneath the lettering for that step. The following explanations give an idea of what should be typed under each heading on the backboard.

1. PROBLEM: Type the problem stated in a clear and concise manner.

2. HYPOTHESIS: Type the hypothesis, the best educated guess which gives the experiment direction. Be certain to include this step whether you proved or disproved your hypothesis.

3. MATERIALS: Type all the items used in the project.

4. PROCEDURE: Type the detailed step-by-step explanations of the experimental process.

5. RESULTS: Type observations pertaining to the experiment and include charts, graphs, and maps.

6. CONCLUSION: Type your interpretations of the results. They should be compared and discussed.

Once these steps are typed, carefully crop them around the typed print and neatly mat them on a solid colored piece of paper so that they stand out and can be read quickly and easily by the judges.

PICTURES AND GRAPHS

If graphs are used to help explain the results of the experiment, it is best to use colors to differentiate the components of the graph. For example, on a bar graph there may be different colored bars. On a line graph there may be different colored lines. Also, use clearly explained legends designed to identify the various parts of the graph. Again, place the graph against a solid colored piece of paper so that the extra color will allow it to stand out and be seen easily.

If you took photographs during the experiment, use these in the display to further explain the project. Display a few of the very best shots that truly provide an illustration for the experiment. Remember not to clutter the backboard with too may photographs.

APPARATUS

If the apparatus used in the experiment is small, then display it in front of the backboard. For example, the 24-hour appliance timer could be set in front of the backboard for display in the "It's TV Time" experiment. Another example of this would be setting the battery, beaker, and test tube apparatus used in the "Parting the Waters" experiment in front of the backboard. The carbon dioxide generating apparatus in the "Talking to Plants" experiment could also be used as a display, as well as showing an unused insect trap from the "Checking-In Creepy Crawlers" experiment.

If the apparatus is too large to actually display, then be certain that there are some photographs of it to place on the display of the project. For example, photographs of the large colored boxes used in the "Plant Lights" experiment would be a helpful visual for judges and other science fair goers. Another example is a photograph of the grow lights and their placement in the "Plant Nap" experiment. A photograph of the filling station in the "Gasoline Alley" experiment would also serve as an appropriate visual aid.

THE REPORT

The entire completed report should be typed and placed in a clear plastic portfolio cover. A portfolio cover gives a neat and professional appearance to the report. The portfolio should be placed in front of the backboard.

The report should begin with a cover page that includes the title and author. All six steps of the scientific method used for the experiment should be included in the report. Additionally, all charts and graphs should be included in the report, as well as maps, if appropriate.

The report should also include any research information that was done for the experiment. Always include the citations of any facts or details that are gathered for a project. If you conduct an experiment that is related to issues about the environment (there are several in this book), you may have found important information from other resources, such as recycling publications. It is important to cite them as they are used. For example, one very informative book about the environment is

50 Simple Things Kids Can Do to Recycle, by Earth Works Press, 1400 Shattuck Avenue #25, Berkeley, California 94709.

When possible, try to seek out published material that supports the hypothesis of the experiment. Research activities can greatly enhance the believability of experimental findings.

THE COMPLETED PROJECT

When complete, the science fair project should be neat and thorough. It should be displayed in an organized way so that judges can find needed information quickly and easily.

The example below is a completed project set up for viewing by judges and others at the science fair. Most important, enjoy the science fair!

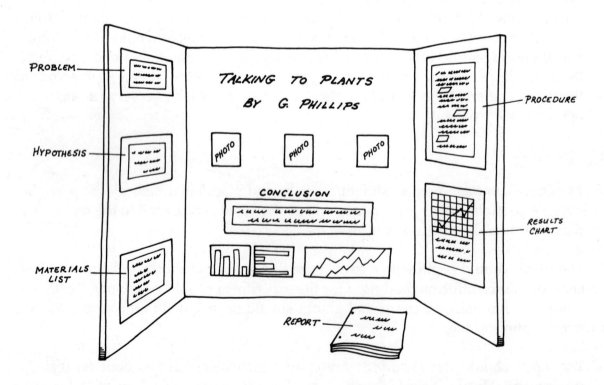

SCIENCE RESOURCES

Listed below are addresses and phone numbers of science companies and catalogs. Many of them have been used in the various experiments in this book. These companies offer a wealth of information, including helpful hints, for obtaining the supplies needed to perform effective science fair experiments.

Brock Optical, Inc.
414 Lake Howell Road
Maitland, FL 32751
Phone 1-800-780-9111 or 407-647-6611
FAX 407-647-1811

Carolina Biological Supply Company
2700 York Road
Burlington, NC 27215
Phone 1-800-334-5551
FAX 1-800-222-7112

Central Scientific Company (CENCO)
3300 CENCO Parkway
Franklin Park, IL 60131
Phone 1-800-262-3626
FAX 1-800-814-0607
Internet http://www.cenconet.com

Connecticut Valley Biological
82 Valley Road
P. O. Box 326
Southampton, MA 01073
Phone 1-800-628-7748
FAX 1-800-355-6813

Fisher Science Education
485 South Frontage Road
Burr Ridge, IL 60521
Phone 1-800-955-1177
FAX 1-800-955-0740
Internet http://www. fisheredu.com

Forestry Suppliers, Inc.
205 West Rankin Street
P. O. Box 8397
Jackson, MS 39284-8397

Frey Scientific
100 Paragon Parkway
P. O. Box 8101
Mansfield, OH 44901-8101
Phone 1-800-225-FREY
FAX   419-589-1522

Nasco Science   or   Nasco Science
901 Janesville Avenue   4825 Stoddard Road
Fort Atkinson, WI 53538-0901   Modesto, CA 95356-9318
Phone 1-800-558-9595   Phone 1-800-558-9595
FAX   414-563-8296   FAX   209-545-1669

Vee Gee Scientific, Inc.
13600 NE 126th Place, Suite A
Kirkland, WA 98034
Phone 1-800-423-8842 or 206-823-4518
FAX   206-820-9826
E-Mail veegee@wolfenet.com

Ward's Biology
P.O. Box 92912
Rochester, NY 14692-9012
Phone 1-800-635-8439
FAX   1-800-962-2660

Internet sites are also helpful resources for teachers and students. Browsing the
Internet for regional or state science fairs may reveal some useful information. The
following Internet address can be used as a starter point.

http://wxvw. scienceworld.bc.ca/Science Fair/SFAbout.HTML

There is also a site, listed below, that is attempting to provide a comprehensive
summary of every science fair. It gives national, state, and regional science fair
information. It also has some specific information for science fair participants that is
helpful.

http://physics.usc.edu/~gould/ScienceFairs